T0371897

PRAISE FOR
OUTSMART THE MONEY MAGICIANS

Manske shows there's a lot more than meets the eye to the simplest parts of finance, like the investment statement and how to save. His book demonstrates that if we change our perspective, we change our results.

> —**J. Bradley Green**, CEO, Park Lawn Corporation,
> the largest publicly traded, Canadian-owned funeral
> services provider

These are complex subjects, and Manske makes them simple and easy to understand. Recommended for all levels of experience.

> —**Mary Perkins**, CFO, Petrocom Energy Group

Manske demonstrates that once we know how an illusion is created, we can't be tricked anymore. With this book, he gives readers more control over their financial destiny. I wholeheartedly recommend it!

> —**Angela (Evans) Gildea**, U.S. National Sector Leader
> for Energy, KPMG

Manske has proved he's a top-notch writer and storyteller. I highly recommend his book to anyone who wants the inside scoop on how to tilt finance so it's not all to Wall Street's advantage.

> —**Frank Toman**, owner, Allstate Insurance Agency, retired

Manske's writing is influential because it empowers the reader and gives people the insight to see the same old thing a new way. With this new outlook, people can't help but understand their finances better.

> —**Anthony Colombo**, President, MC2 Civil, providing
> construction and oilfield services for various municipalities
> and the Texas Department of Transportation

Christopher Manske is a powerful voice in finance, and his latest book shows his relentless focus on taking care of the investing client.
—**Tim Phillips**, President & CEO, Revenade, offering global organizational consulting

This book tells us what the establishment won't, and Manske is the perfect financial expert to lay it all out clearly. Read it!
—**Robert Lopez**, Thunderbird School of Global Management, MBA, and Director of Engineering, Cameron International, retired

Are we saving enough money? Are we paying too much in taxes? Manske shows us why these questions keep arising and how to truly answer them once and for all. What a great book!
—**Patrick Schweitzer**, Distinguished Engineering Associate, ExxonMobil Research & Engineering

This is a must-read for anyone who feels they can save more but aren't. As an advisor myself managing about $150 million, I know that both investment experts and people new to the field will appreciate Manske's message.
—**Elijah Lopez**, Senior Investment Advisor and Certified Financial Planner

This is a financial expert exposing the tricks of the trade, and Manske's book is an excellent resource for anyone trying to get ahead financially.
—**Jerold Coker**, owner, Geico Insurance Agency

OUTSMART THE MONEY MAGICIANS

ALSO BY CHRISTOPHER MANSKE

The Prepared Investor: How to Prevent the Next Crisis from Affecting Your Financial Independence

OUTSMART *THE* MONEY MAGICIANS

MAXIMIZE YOUR NET WORTH
BY SEEING THROUGH
THE MOST POWERFUL ILLUSIONS
PERFORMED BY
WALL STREET AND THE IRS

CHRISTOPHER MANSKE, CFP®

NEW YORK   CHICAGO   SAN FRANCISCO   ATHENS   LONDON
MADRID   MEXICO CITY   MILAN   NEW DELHI
SINGAPORE   SYDNEY   TORONTO

1 2 3 4 5 6 7 8 9 LCR 28 27 26 25 24 23

ISBN   978-1-265-43296-6
MHID   1-265-43296-1

e-ISBN 978-1-265-43332-1
e-MHID   1-265-43332-1

This publication is designed to provide accurate and authoritative information in regard to the subject matter covered. It is sold with the understanding that neither the author nor the publisher is engaged in rendering legal, accounting, securities trading, or other professional services. If legal advice or other expert assistance is required, the services of a competent professional person should be sought.

—From a Declaration of Principles Jointly Adopted by a Committee of the American Bar Association and a Committee of Publishers and Associations

Library of Congress Cataloging-in-Publication Data

Names: Manske, Christopher R., author.
Title: Outsmart the money magicians : maximize your net worth by seeing
    through the most powerful illusions performed by Wall Street and the IRS
    / by Christopher Manske, CFP.
Description: New York : McGraw Hill, [2023]
Identifiers: LCCN 2023034374 (print) | LCCN 2023034375 (ebook) | ISBN
    9781265432966 (hardback) | ISBN 9781265433321 (ebook)
Subjects: LCSH: Finance, Personal. | Money—Psychological aspects.
Classification: LCC HG179 .M265 2023 (print) | LCC HG179 (ebook) |
    DDC 332.024—dc23/eng/20230726
LC record available at https://lccn.loc.gov/2023034374
LC ebook record available at https://lccn.loc.gov/2023034375

I gratefully dedicate this book to the seven authors who have most influenced my writing and my life. Please email me at cmanske@manskewealth.com so I may share their names and my list of "Required Reading for All Humans."

CONTENTS

PART TWO

THE THEATER, DECONSTRUCTED

INTRODUCTION

"I've been saving for so long! It doesn't seem right that this is all I have to show for it."

"When my investment statement arrives, I don't even open it. Even if I go online, I can't easily see what they are charging me or the performance of my overall portfolio."

"I know people make more money than me, but they're paying less taxes than me. How can I pay the IRS less? I feel like the system is rigged."

With over 20 years in finance as a money manager and leader of financial advisors, I've heard statements like these a lot. I've written this book to shine a light on why people often feel like they don't have control of their money or their financial future. It's not because they aren't intelligent or don't have enough finance experience. It's because there are specific ways the system actually is rigged and distorted so that our perception of our money is manipulated, very similar to how a stage magician does illusions. And also, like those stage tricks, these financial manipulations are easy to see through with just a little bit of education and focus.

Outsmart the Money Magicians answers, "How'd they do that?" by offering clarity on the five biggest, most widely accepted financial distortions happening every day all over America. Each of these financial illusions is systemic and pervasive, and most people are not even aware that their perception is being manipulated. If you've ever thought that it shouldn't be so hard to examine your investment portfolio or hold your financial advisor accountable, you're right. The system distorts your view of your money in the same way that a magician stacks the deck against the audience. It's not evil or bad, but once you know how the magician does the illusion, you simply cannot be tricked so easily anymore. And once we all are in on the trick, the financial industry will need to improve, because the old, tired illusions won't work anymore.

In this book, I describe the IRS and Wall Street as tricksters and illusionists—the Money Magicians—because they are successfully distracting Main Street and distorting our view of our money. Deception and misdirection are acceptable in a magic show, but they are not at all appropriate in the arena of finance. The way we look at our investments and what we see when we examine our portfolios are both important because our view determines how well we navigate toward our financial goals. When individuals perceive their money accurately, the path to success is a lot shorter and easier. If you have come to this book, you might be seeking a clearer view of your finances. Perhaps you wonder if you've missed some opportunities for advancement and achievement. Maybe you'd like to gain more control over your financial future.

To understand how this book will help you win back control over your money, let's visit the African savannah where the sun shines bright and the dry wind whispers through tall yellow grass. The occasional acacia tree provides some shade as lions, gazelles, and other animals seek their food and water. Those trees all consume carbon dioxide and give off oxygen. This is not a good or bad thing. It simply is. The lions hunt and eat the gazelles. The great predators hide in the yellow grass, upwind from the herd, and strike when their prey has wandered close. For the lions to survive, they need to eat the gazelle, so it's natural for predators to hide upwind from their prey.

But from the gazelle's perspective, this system seems rigged. Each time a lion almost magically appears out of the yellow grass, the gazelles wonder, "How'd he do that?" Imagine if the herd of gazelles could somehow understand the problem lurking in the tall yellow grass. They'd think, "The lion is tricking us by hiding in that yellow grass! We can't see the predator there, so he's taking advantage of us on purpose!" Once they know the lion didn't magically appear out of nowhere, they'll never go near the tall yellow grass again. And just like that, things would change. It doesn't mean the lions won't survive nor that another gazelle will not be eaten. It doesn't mean the African savannah system as a whole has been broken. It's just that the scales would be slightly more balanced, and it would be harder for the lions to fool the gazelles.

The American financial system has its own lions and gazelles. If Wall Street and the IRS are the lions, then the regular everyday investor on Main Street is the gazelle. Thankfully, this isn't a story about people getting eaten, but it's valuable to think about how the brokerage firms and the tax man survive. Transactions, investment activity, consumerism . . . these are the food of the financial lions. If nobody bought a single stock at all, the stock market would grind to a halt and the system would be broken. Transactions are the lifeblood of that system. If people didn't buy and consume goods and services, it would be very difficult for the IRS to collect taxes.

The fact that Wall Street and the IRS require transactions and consumerism is, by itself, not a bad thing. They are not the evil villain in this story, but if you're a gazelle, it is very helpful to know how their regulations might be encouraging (or for the more cynical, manipulating) you to do unnecessary transactions. It's certainly useful to know how Main Street is being helped (duped) into consuming goods and services when most regular investors would behave differently given a clear understanding of the danger hiding in the grass.

No matter your politics, goals, or level of wealth, this book is a systemic call to action, because after you read it, you will not save money the way you do now. You won't look at investment statements or your performance reports the way you do now. If enough people stop wandering near the tall yellow grass, the US financial system itself could be forced to improve, because the lions will be forced to change their ways. Regulations themselves will need to change, because we'll all understand how the game we're playing right now is rigged against us in devious yet meaningful ways.

Once you know how an illusion is performed, you cannot go back to being tricked by it. Growing your financial stability isn't some scary esoteric business that you need to get a PhD to understand. You don't need to keep giving money and power to people who don't have your best interest in mind, and in a way, you already know that. For example, we use our cell phones for hours every single day even though we really don't have a deep understanding of how the technology actually works. One of the reasons we are comfortable with our phone might be the fact that cell phone companies aren't trying to pull one over on us. Just the opposite. Apple, for example, has a reputation for being so helpful and customer-focused that it has a famously loyal clientele.

Just like we can learn the myriad of new ways to use a cell phone beyond just calling someone, we are capable of reading and understanding how to save and grow our financial security, regardless of the technical intricacies that make the system work. Main Street can interpret basic data. We can do critical thinking. And we certainly can do these things while partnering with the right financial experts who truly have our best interests in mind.

Somehow, individual investors have accepted that we cannot avoid going near the tall yellow grass. Main Street has fallen into the trap of believing that financial security is like some magic show where only the magicians on stage know what's really going on. *Outsmart the Money Magicians* will help you escape that trap and improve your financial well-being. This book shows you how to avoid the lion's hiding spot so you can maximize your net worth. In the process, you'll come to see through the biggest, most powerful illusions performed by Wall Street and the IRS.

OUTSMART *THE* MONEY MAGICIANS

PART ONE

THE ILLUSIONS, EXPLAINED

WHAT'S INSIDE

How the system tricks people into:

- Spending more than they should
- Lowering their own net worth
- Misunderstanding performance and buying overly risky investments
- Misunderstanding profit versus loss and selling investments worth keeping
- Seeking deductions for tax purposes that decrease their ability to save

Each chapter in Part One begins with a familiar magic trick performed by an actual stage magician. The stage magician astounds the audience with devices and techniques that are very similar to (if not exactly the same as) the methods of the Money Magicians. *Spoiler alert:* You will discover how magicians perform their stage magic! After you know how the magician did that chapter's trick on stage, I'll describe a financial illusion performed by Wall Street and/or the IRS as Main Street typically experiences it. Then, I'll pull back the curtain to explain how the Money Magicians did it so you can't be duped in the future.

In the first chapter, you'll learn how the system tricks people into spending more than they should. If you've ever said, "I pay myself first!" or "I'm a good saver because I set it and forget it," then this illusion is affecting you right now because you think the "it" in that statement is your savings. But you shouldn't be setting your savings, because this ruse is the foundation for lifestyle creep, keeping up with the Joneses, and being a consumer instead of a saver.

Next, we explore wealth versus income. I ask readers to remember why they buy investments in the first place. Wall Street works hard to make sure we focus on growing our net worth, but is that truly our goal? Is "more and more" really the answer, or are you being tricked into being a consumer who asks the wrong questions? We'll discuss how people get manipulated into owning things that lower their net worth because they think it signals success. This is the "profit-by-sale" mentality and will be very helpful to anyone who has ever said, "I'll just flip it!" or "I'll turn around and sell it for more than I paid."

In Chapter 3, the illusion centers on investment performance. Sadly, actual profit often is not the same as reported profit. If you've ever heard friends brag about their portfolio's return while you wished your portfolio was doing better, then you'll enjoy learning about how Wall Street takes advantage of our natural tendency to gravitate toward an easy measurement even if it's wrong and misleading. That easy, but wrong, measurement is average annual return, and it's one of Wall Street's biggest illusions.

For the fourth illusion, we'll focus on the way Wall Street reports to Main Street and discuss how the IRS has influenced the data you see when you examine your finances. You will see how investment statements systemically distort your understanding of both profit and loss by using data known as "cost basis." That distortion is incredibly powerful because this illusion can trick you into thinking investments are performing poorly, which often leads to selling (more transactions).

In the final illusion to finish out Part One, we'll discuss tax brackets and why it's so wrong, yet so common, to hear people say, "I don't want to be in the highest tax bracket," or "I need to buy some things I can deduct so I don't have such a high tax bill this year." We'll see how everyday investors on Main Street regularly get tricked into spending money that's rightfully theirs to save. This chapter is for anyone who has ever said, "I don't want the IRS to get any more of my money," or "At this point, I thought I'd have more savings."

Let the show begin!

THE QUARTER
AND THE CUP TRICK

Where Did All
Your Savings Go?

You have won a coveted front-row VIP seat to the greatest magic show on earth. Your backstage pass, a thick, round metal talisman, hangs around your neck and is inscribed with the words "All Powerful" over a picture of a top hat with a bull emerging from inside. When you enter the theater to see the show, the people who work there defer to you with their eyes slightly wide as they steal glimpses at your VIP medallion. One of the ushers guides you along the plush dark carpet to your front-row seat beneath the dimming lights recessed in the vaulted ceilings.

Your special pass grants total authority over the show. You can stop the performance at any time and approach the stage and examine everything the magician is doing. What's more, you can ask whatever question you like of the magician and his assistants, and they must answer truthfully. Sitting in front of the heavy red curtain that conceals the stage, you finger the cold amulet, waiting for the show to begin. Your excited anticipation is only surpassed by your sense of purpose because, tonight, nothing will stop you from answering the question, "How'd he do that?"

THE ONSTAGE PERFORMANCE— WHERE DID THE MONEY GO?

The lights go down until the entire theater is in darkness. The magician materializes just a few feet away from you as if even his arrival is something unexplainable. He's wearing the famous black top hat with a white shirt, and he's got on a cape with a red satin underside. When he looks out into the audience, you sense him looking directly at you as he directs everyone's attention to three upside-down plastic cups on a table beside him.

"Magicians the world over love to make people's money disappear because it's an easy way to raise tension and arouse curiosity," says the magician mysteriously as he lifts one of the plastic cups for all to see. He continues, "Everyone understands money is valuable and it's bad for it to disappear. For my first trick, I'm going to need a volunteer." You hold up your metal VIP pass, and the magician immediately tips his hat to you.

Looking you in the eye, the magician asks for a quarter, and you fish one out of your pocket for him. He takes out a black marker and asks you to mark the quarter in a unique way, so you put a large letter M on it. He puts the marked coin on top of the table alongside the three upside-down cups. One of the cups is red, one is green, and the last one is blue. Keeping your eye on the quarter, you watch the magician deliberately place it under the red cup. Then, he begins to slowly move the cups around the table.

While always moving the cups in various patterns on the table, he says, "It should be very easy for you to find your quarter because you know it is under the red cup. But I'll make it even easier for you.

Let's get rid of one of the empty cups so you have a 50-50 chance to find your quarter. Should I get rid of the blue or the green one," he asks while, with his wand, he taps the top of the blue cup and green cup, respectively. You select the blue one, and he lifts it up and tosses it away.

As he continues to move the red and green cups around at a slightly faster rate, the magician smiles. "I will help you even more," he says as he picks up the green cup and tosses it to the side as well. He moves the red cup to the middle of the table.

"OK, where is your money?" he asks. You point to the only cup on the table.

"Go ahead and lift the red cup," he says. But when you lift it up, the table is bare. You look inside the cup as well, but the fact is, your quarter is gone. It's magic! The magician then leans toward you with an expression of wonder as if he too is witnessing the impossible. He reaches out and takes something out of your ear. You can see the black letter M you wrote on it earlier. It's your quarter! You were watching the whole time, and yet, somehow, he got your quarter out from under that cup and found it, of all places, in your ear!

THE ALL-POWERFUL VIP PASS— CONSTANT VERSUS VARIABLE ON STAGE

You ask the question the audience also wonders, "How'd you do that?" The magician frowns, but with your VIP pass held high, you know he must explain the entire trick.

"Are you sure you want to know this?" he asks. "Once you know how a trick is done, you can never enjoy it again. The awe, the mystery, the magic itself will be gone. You can never go back to how it was."

But this is why you're here. Pierce the veil. False awe is just a gentle way to describe manipulation. A mystery that is only fabricated for the purpose of fooling someone else is trickery of the worst kind. The magician sees your resolve and signals to his assistant to describe what really happened.

It turns out, the assistant explains, that misdirection and timing are very important factors contributing to this illusion. It begins by creating a known constant, something that is accepted as true and relied upon over time. In this case, it's the fact that the quarter is under the red cup. Then comes the misdirection. When the magician asked you to "pick a cup to toss aside," he tapped the tops of the plastic cups to naturally draw your attention to them for the briefest second. It was an important part of the trick, because when you made that selection, there was a brief moment when your attention was not on the red cup. It's in that moment when the entire trick happens, though only the magician knows it. He had smoothly moved the red cup just a little bit off the edge of the table so that the quarter fell into his lap.

That specific point in time is important because it's when everything changes. Everything that matters has shifted without the audience being aware of it, and the magician encourages that feeling by prolonging the trick. Time continues to go by, the cups are still moving around on the table, and people believe the situation is still the same as it was. The quarter under the red cup is viewed as a constant, even though the truth is that it's variable. It moved!

Palming the quarter from his own lap and "grabbing" it from your ear was an easy conclusion to the illusion. Everything in this simple but powerful trick relies on two things: the misplaced belief in a constant and time continuing to pass by while that constant (which was actually variable) has changed.

OUTSIDE THE THEATER

This same kind of trick happens to almost everyone, every day, in real life. Just like the quarter that disappeared from under the red cup, people often look at their savings accounts and wonder, "Where is the money? I've been saving for years, but this is all I have?" In the real world, we accept a system, like a table with three cups on it, and we miss the moment when things change and the quarter is no longer where we think it is.

As an advisor to both clients and other investment advisors, I have heard this far too many times: "We make a lot of money, but it seems like we're not holding onto it." "I know I make a good salary and I'm saving properly, so why does it seem like I don't have much money?" Wall Street loves tricking us into spending more and saving less. Before I pull back the curtain on this powerful illusion, let's examine what normally happens and then we will pierce the veil.

THE REAL-LIFE PERFORMANCE— WHERE DID THE MONEY GO?

Ron and Sally got married a couple of years ago and just had a baby boy they named Mikey. Ron works at the bank, and Sally works part-time as a lawyer. Together, they make about $100,000 per year. When Ron and Sally were first married and Mikey wasn't born yet, the two of them agreed to save 12 percent of their income each year, which was about $1,000 per month. Now with Mikey entering the picture, they save another $250 per month for Mikey's college fund.

At Mikey's first birthday, one of Sally's close friends asks how she and Ron are saving for the future. Sally explains that they're saving 12 percent of their income and a little more for Mikey's future college costs.

Sally says, "We put this together years ago. You know—set it and forget it."

Ron adds, "That's right! You know how everyone says you need to pay yourself first? That's what we do! Every month, the first bill we pay is a thousand dollars to our savings and then a bit more for our son's future. It's automatic so we don't even have to do anything."

When Mikey turns five years old, Sally and Ron meet with a stockbroker who congratulates them on being so disciplined all these years. "Most people can't stick to a savings plan," he says. "But you two have done a great job. You've made your future more secure by continuing to set aside the same amount every month. I'm so glad to have the opportunity to work with you." The stockbroker suggests buying and selling various investments to help them grow their net worth.

Later, when their son is in the eighth grade, Sally and Ron take a vacation alone at the beach to celebrate 15 years of marriage. On the first evening of that vacation, they enjoy talking about their life together as they watch the sun go down over the ocean's waves. Ron's now a vice president at the bank, and Sally is a partner at a prestigious law firm. They own a beautiful home, and each drives a luxury car. But while there's plenty of money coming in, they're both frustrated that their savings and investment accounts don't seem to have changed much.

Ron admits, "After 15 years, I thought we'd have a lot more by now."

Sally replies, "It seems like everyone around us is so well off, and I know we make a lot of money. It just feels like we're living paycheck to paycheck and that, even though there's more money coming in, we're not really leaping ahead like I thought."

That conversation was the moment they lifted up their red cup and wondered, "Why isn't there anything there?" And they are right. They aren't leaping ahead the way they should. They have an itch; they have an instinctual knowledge that it's not going right, but they can't put their finger on how the trick was done.

Something changed, and time kept marching by without their being aware of an important misdirection. Though they set up their finances the way all the experts suggest, Ron and Sally can tell they missed something along the way. They've been tricked into being consumers, which means their lifestyle has crept up as the years went by. Here's the secret behind this trick and why it's so destructive to a family's net worth over the long term.

THE ALL-POWERFUL VIP PASS—CONSTANT VERSUS VARIABLE IN REAL LIFE

This illusion centers on the ideology, "Save 10 percent of your income. Just set it and forget it. Pay yourself first." Stop being fooled. Ron and Sally are doing what most Americans do, and it's terribly flawed. They go to work, and most of their pay is deposited into their checking account at the bank. Some of their earnings gets taken out before they receive their deposit because of taxes, insurance, and maybe a company benefit. The rest of the money gets sent automatically to their checking account—which they use to pay all their bills and other expenses. As they said, the first bill they pay at the start of each month is $1,000 to their future and then $250 to their son's college account. They committed to the philosophy "Set it and forget it," where they move funds away from their checking account so those monies are "out of sight, out of mind."

This savings setup is like the system of colored cups being shuffled on a table. Ron and Sally know for sure that the quarter is under the red cup just like they know for sure that they set aside their money into savings. "Set it and forget it" also means that, mentally, they feel as though they have successfully accomplished the task of saving. They treat it like a constant. The saving is automatically done. The need to address their financial future is complete. The quarter is there under the red cup, so they don't need to keep thinking about saving. In fact, the famous saying ends with the command to "forget it."

"Pay yourself first" is a misdirection away from what that philosophy means for the rest of Ron and Sally's money. The prescription suggests that since they have already saved, naturally everything else in the checking account is available to be spent. "Out of sight, out of mind" actually encourages people to spend, spend, spend because they have completed the task of saving.

This philosophy of "Pay yourself first" is a powerful trick because Wall Street convinced Ron and Sally to lock in their savings every month. As a natural consequence, this made their lifestyle variable. A variable lifestyle means you could spend more money next month than this month while your fixed savings remains steadfast and unchanged. They saved their $1,000 and then spent the rest on things like nice cars and fancy vacations.

It's a siren song that most people are drawn to because they like the idea of "the good life" and want to signal to their community that they are upwardly mobile. Culturally, it's very "American" to move a number of times because your "starter home" would never be your home for life. It's hard to believe there was a time when Americans bought a home, slowly paid off the mortgage, and basically stayed there for almost their whole life.

This entire illusion rests on the Money Magicians convincing us that our financial lives are constant instead of variable. Ron and Sally are a great example because they, like most other Americans, collect a salary. This makes them think that their lifestyle isn't really all that variable. Most people believe, "My lifestyle is about the same every month. Our savings are fixed. We make a salary, so what we earn is fixed. And lastly, what we spend is fixed." But the truth is that no one reading this book has a robotic life filled with endless repeating loops where they get paid the exact same amount of money every single month for decades on end. We all have fluctuations in our income, just like the cups on the magician's table aren't moving around in the exact same patterns.

At some point, the red cup slides a bit off the table, and the money situation is different. In real life, everyone experiences a moment—probably a lot of moments—when the money coming in is a bit more or less for a variety of normal reasons. But we don't catch that truth and identify it as the important change that it is, just like we don't see the quarter disappear into the magician's lap.

Here are some examples of how people's income streams can change. Maybe Ron and Sally have a garage sale. Maybe they earn a bonus from work. Maybe they get a check as a gift for their birthday from a loved one. But the most common change that everyone is working toward is a promotion at work. With "Set it and forget it," what typically happens is that all these extra dollars get spent, which creates a problem known as "lifestyle creep." It's the natural result of fixing your savings: Your lifestyle becomes variable and sucks up all the extra money.

For Ron and Sally, they've had a lot of the normal American family accomplishments that would make anyone feel proud. For example, in the last five years, Sally earned some overtime compensation on a big legal case. Ron earned a couple of nice bonuses from the bank. They had a garage sale that made some money. Ron also collected a bit more extra pay as a Little League coach. During those same five years, Ron and Sally together had three different promotions at their respective jobs.

What happened to all that extra money? Every month of those last five years, Ron and Sally moved $1,000 plus $250 "out of sight, out of mind," which meant everything else in the checking account was allowed to be spent. I think it's fair to say that they tried to make good choices along the way, and on occasion, they put a few extra dollars toward savings. But the point is that they didn't feel the need to save because they thought the quarter was under the red cup. When they got a promotion or collected money during the garage sale, they missed the importance of that moment. They missed it because they had already "set it" and were happy to "forget it" while they spent all the extra funds.

Their lifestyle crept up because this trick fools people into thinking that they've already saved. Ron and Sally were going through their daily lives believing that the requirement to save had already been met. Whenever Ron earned an extra bonus or a family member sent Sally money, they didn't realize that something had changed. They didn't notice the quarter slipping off the table, because the cups just kept circling as if nothing special had happened. Unfortunately, the bonus money and the family gift are in the checking account, and since they've already saved, Ron and Sally are left wondering why their lives cost so much and yet they have so little.

"Set it and forget it" is a powerful trick that encourages people to be consumers, and over time, they allow their lifestyles to creep up. You know you're dealing with lifestyle creep when you buy more and more things that make your need for money go up, such as getting a bigger house with bigger utility bills (we'll explore this more in Chapter 2). Let's all consider that when we see someone with a fancy car, we aren't seeing wealth or status. We're seeing proof the person does not have that money in his possession anymore!

When you give your money to a restaurant or a retail store, the goods you get in return might show others something of your financial means, but it also depletes your wealth. You're showing people that you *used* to have money and now you have something that costs more money. The car is just a reflection of wealth rather than actual wealth, and it's easier to fall into this trap when people lock in their savings at some amount per month (for Ron and Sally, it was $1,000). That's better than doing nothing, but what happens to the rest of their money as it sits in the checking account?

This system promotes "keeping up with the Jones family" and ensures lifestyle creep instead of encouraging the stability and security that comes from getting out of debt and saving your money. Even if you change your savings amount after each promotion, there are still a lot of variable funds that slip through the cracks. As people spend what is available, they are actually living paycheck to paycheck. Falling for this magician's act almost guarantees that you will be less wealthy and less financially secure over time. There is another way.

WHAT TO DO: AVOID THE SYSTEM, AVOID THE PROBLEMS

At its core, this powerful trick is a ridiculously simple one, which means it's also easy to correct. The illusion requires that people lock in their savings, and so to upend this, you just need to do the opposite. Lock in your lifestyle instead, which means you commit to a budget instead of a specific savings amount.

Most people think it's hard to stick with a budget, but you can easily take control of growing your net worth by setting your savings free and fixing your lifestyle. We've all heard stories of "the millionaire next door" and "slow and steady wins the race," but we've gotten away from those simple truths because of the siren song of a fancy car and a bigger house and the false promise that "Pay yourself first" works. If you lock in your lifestyle, you are separating from the people who are trying to keep up with their neighbors. Let them try to turn all their wealth into cars, purses, and extra air conditioners for their overly large homes.

What is this easy method to lock in your lifestyle? Is there an effective way to make your savings variable and your lifestyle fixed? The answer is a resounding yes! And it's incredibly simple.

ACTION STEP: Make all the money coming into your life go directly to your savings account first.

You can become the millionaire next door with one simple change: Do not let any money in your life go directly to your checking account. That's it! Almost all the people you know make most of their deposits go directly into a checking account including their monthly pay. Whenever people have extra money for whatever reason, it usually goes into the checking account, making it the main operating account where they pay their bills. Any time people set up fund-sharing systems like Venmo, it's all connected to the checking account. To lift the red cup and find your quarter again, all you need to do is the opposite of this. Simply make all incoming funds from every possible source go to your savings account first.

To make all payments and incoming funds go to your savings account first, you'll need to tell your job to change your direct deposit so it goes into your savings. When you receive money from a garage sale or a side business or when a family member gives you a gift, just be sure to deposit it directly into your savings account. Nothing should ever go from the outside world directly into your checking account.

After you have established your savings account as the first stop for every payment you can possibly receive, you've brilliantly and effectively captured all the future fluctuation in your monetary situation. When you get your next promotion, those extra funds will already be in your savings account because that's where every cent you make goes. When you get a bonus or sell a car, those funds are all in savings right from the start. Nothing gets lost to lifestyle creep because every cent is in savings. This is truly taking control of your finances, and sadly, very few Americans do it.

ACTION STEP: Create a monthly allowance to cover your bills and control your lifestyle.

With everything going to savings, we have a small problem, because there's nothing in your checking account. In order to pay your bills and live your life, you simply need to create a fixed, automatic payment that happens once or twice a month. It's a specific amount of money that makes sense to you and your family that moves from your savings into your checking account. You now have accomplished something very powerful: You have a fixed lifestyle and variable savings, as opposed to Ron and Sally who had fixed their savings and spent the rest.

You created your own budget, and you're paying it out like clockwork. No funds from the outside world make it directly to your checking account, so anything beyond that budgeted amount is automatically saved. If you can set aside the little bit of time needed to do this, you will have done a "Set it and forget it" to your *lifestyle*. No more keeping up with the Jones family!

Each month, regardless of how much money you've got coming in from various sources, you can be certain that the amount available for your family to spend is exactly the same. Month after month, year after year, you can successfully "pay yourself first" by *truly* doing just that. Wall Street corrupted that saying by hinting that saving for the future and growing your net worth is just a side bill that gets paid before the rest of your bills. But when we pull back the curtain, the audience can see that the real meaning of "Pay yourself first" is the act of setting a limit on your lifestyle and removing the limits on how much you can save.

You can expect that, over time, your savings account will keep getting larger and larger. This is because any variability in your financial life is captured as savings. Instead of your lifestyle creeping up because you keep spending the extra, your net worth creeps up instead. All those extra dollars stay in savings, which means they don't go into the checking account. The only way you'd spend some of that savings is if you go out of your way to purposefully make a withdrawal.

You are going to be surprised at how much money used to slip through your fingers as you watch your extra savings build up every month. As the years go by and you get promotions and bonuses, the extra funds will start growing a whole lot faster. Nothing good comes easy, and you won't raise a million dollars overnight. However, by keeping your lifestyle in check, you will be on a clear path toward a wealthier and stronger financial position.

This system helps make sure you are not enticed to spend money on things you really don't need. It puts you in control of your budget because you've set your monthly spending limit and made your lifestyle a withdrawal from your savings account. It's almost impossible to experience lifestyle creep and wonder where it all went. Just the opposite occurs. Your savings account creeps up in value, and you'll find yourself wondering how you've got so much!

ACTION STEP: Set a "high-water mark" for your savings account so that any money above that line goes directly toward your long-term goals.

By sending everything you earn to savings first, you have answered the question, "How do I create an emergency savings account?" Wall Street often says that you should have three to six months of cash on hand for emergency purposes. Identify that high-water mark for your savings account. Once you have your emergency money saved up in your savings account, you can use the extra funds above that amount to make investments that will grow your net worth and accomplish the goals in life that truly matter to you.

Setting that high-water mark on your savings helps to make it clear how much of your savings account is available for investing and other goals. But beware! What exactly should you buy with that extra money? You've successfully stopped yourself from engaging in lifestyle creep, but how do you take the next step toward maximizing your net worth? There are a lot of different ways to strategically use your extra funds, and this question takes us to the next major illusion performed by the Money Magicians, which I call the "Hall of Mirrors."

DISILLUSION

THERE ARE ONLY FOUR REASONS TO HIRE A FINANCIAL ADVISOR

When the system is set up well, investment advisors offer a valuable service that can be positively life-changing. In a book that points out multiple ways the system is *not* set up well, it's worth it to offer some clarity on when it makes sense to engage with a financial advisor. The reality is that not all people need to pay someone else to take care of their money and do investing for them. In fact, there are only four reasons to hire a financial advisor—and if none of them are applicable, then you should stay away from the extra fees involved with hiring one. On the other hand, if even one of these four reasons applies to you, I suggest reading this entire book and then setting an immediate goal to hire a professional to help you with your money. The four reasons center on capability, desire, time, and care.

CAPABILITY

If you did an honest self-assessment, would you say you have what it takes to manage your finances? Investing your money involves a serious appreciation for math and numbers. Some people are not comfortable with the arithmetic required in money management. But there's more than numbers because investments fluctuate. There's also an emotional component where patience and stoicism are often rewarded, while hot-headedness and fear of loss are punished. If you are confident in your investing capabilities, then you might not need to hire a third party to handle your investing for you.

DESIRE

Do you have the desire to manage your own money? Many people are quite capable of handling their finances, but they find the tasks involved unenjoyable. If you simply detest the work required to keep up with your various investments and accounts, then it doesn't matter how capable you are at the job, because you'll get satisfaction from delegating those requirements to a professional. However, if you enjoy managing money and you feel capable doing it, then you probably do not need to pay an additional fee to an investment advisor.

TIME

Do you have the time to manage your own money? You might enjoy financial management and feel very comfortable doing it, but you might not have the time in your schedule to complete and sustain the job. There are only so many hours in the day, and as you prioritize how you wish to spend your time, you might find that the daily supervision of your investments is lower in the pecking order than spending time with family, friends, career, and physical-spiritual-mental health. In my experience, the vast majority of clients hire professional advisors for this reason. They simply don't wish to devote the time necessary to stay on top of the market changes and administrative details involved with their finances.

CARE

You enjoy managing the family's money and feel capable doing so, but does your spouse? If the answer is no, you'll want to hire a professional, so that if something happens to you, your spouse isn't stuck finding and hiring a money manager or picking up the financial pieces you've left behind. Instead, you establish a relationship with a professional so that your spouse can feel some continuity and security after you're no longer in the driver's seat.

From this perspective, hiring a financial advisor is pretty similar to hiring a lawn service or going to a by-hand car wash. If you can take care of your own yard, and you like doing it, and have the time to do it, then why would you hire a lawn service? If you enjoy washing and waxing your car, you have all the equipment to do so, and it's a beautiful, carefree Saturday afternoon, then why would you pay someone else to do it? If you don't feel comfortable doing these things or you have other more pressing activities to do, then outsourcing to an expert makes a lot of sense.

THE HALL OF MIRRORS TRICK

Is Your Wealth Only a Reflection?

W e're conditioned that our success (and our neighbor's) is best measured by looking at our possessions. Those possessions influence perception, and because a certain perception earns us status, we chase the proof of wealth rather than wealth itself. The Range Rover, the Gucci sunglasses, a particular zip code—all are indications that someone is supposedly financially secure; this is how "keeping up with the Jones family" works. In this system, what you own signals how well you are doing compared with others.

I call it a "system" because Wall Street works hard to keep us focused on the total value of all our possessions—our net worth—rather than on the income our possessions create. For example, two different people can both say they are worth a million dollars, and it might mean very different financial situations. The first person might have a penthouse and two exotic cars. The second person could rent a home, own no cars, and have a million dollars' worth of stock in an investment account. Most people would look at the first person as the wealthier, more successful of the two, but that's an illusion.

What we own—a Ferrari versus a blue-chip mutual fund—is such an important part of financial security, but Wall Street treats all our possessions the same when calculating net worth. This complex deception leads us to believe that someone who is worth $10 million is always better off than someone who is worth $5 million even though we have all heard of fabulously rich celebrities that still end up going broke.

There is a serious trick behind this race for wealth, and the key to understanding this illusion has to do with income. As touched upon in the last chapter, there is a way to structure your income so that you automatically create extra money and more opportunity for your household. For the next step on the path to outsmart the Money Magicians, this chapter answers the question, "What should I use my extra money to buy?"

THE ONSTAGE PERFORMANCE— WHERE IS THE MONEY?

Sitting up front in your VIP chair, you see the magician standing at stage left, lit up in the bright circle of a spotlight in the dark theater. In his hands, he holds a stack of $100 bills, which he casually flips through as he asks the audience, "Where is the money? Can it teleport? Is it even really here?" As he speaks, the spotlight slowly dims until there's total blackness. The entire audience seems to hold its breath until the spotlight reappears now stage right, illuminating the magician. He waves the stack of money as he asks the audience, "Or is the money really over here?"

But there's very little clapping, and you hear someone behind you mutter, "The lights were out for a long time. He probably just ran over there to the right side of the stage." The magician straightens, holding up his hand as if to suggest something is about to happen. The spotlight goes out and almost immediately it illuminates the far left of the stage again, and there is the magician counting his hundreds. *How did he get the money there so fast? Can he teleport?*

Before the audience can clap, the spotlight illuminating the magician at the left of the stage winks out at the exact same time that the spotlight at the right of the stage turns on. There's no way he ran across the stage in the darkness because he instantaneously disappeared and reappeared at the far side of the stage. *It's magic!* The magician's smile glints in the glare of the spotlight, and he puts all the money into his top hat as the audience claps wildly.

THE ALL-POWERFUL VIP PASS— REFLECTION VERSUS THE GENUINE ARTICLE ON STAGE

Using your one-of-a-kind special pass, you immediately stop the show, have a stagehand turn up all the lights in the theater, and approach the stage to learn how the teleport trick works. The first thing you notice is that there are very large mirrors at each side of the theater's stage and a heavy dark curtain in the middle of the stage between them. The audience cannot see behind the curtain, and in the dark, no one even knew the curtain or mirrors were there. As you walk along the stage, you see a set of mirrors that are perfectly positioned so that whatever is behind the curtain will be seen at both the far right and far left side of the theater at the same time.

The magician never moved! Instead, he turned the entire stage into a Hall of Mirrors. In both cases, the audience saw a spotlight illuminating a reflection of the magician and not the actual person. He simply stood behind the curtain while the mirrors projected his image to both the left and right side of the stage simultaneously.

People assumed they saw the actual magician holding real money there at one side of the stage. But the reality is that they only saw a mirror image of him. The audience was duped into thinking something was physically there when it wasn't. What the audience saw was only a reflection and not the genuine article.

The relationship between a reflection and the real thing has a unique characteristic. A reflection of something cannot exist without the real thing to support it. Said another way, a reflection of something is dependent on what's true and real. That means that for the magician's reflection to remain framed in a mirror over time, the actual person is held captive and cannot move. If he got up and moved out of line with the mirrors, then his reflection in the Hall of Mirrors would immediately disappear.

Time, therefore, matters in this trick, because as the moments turn into hours, at some point the magician must move. Whether he goes to the bathroom or wants to go home to his family, his reflection is doomed by the simple fact that the real thing cannot remain trapped in the same place forever. Basically, the reflection maintains its existence at the expense of the genuine article. Or to say it more cynically, the reflection must imprison the real thing so it can continue to exist.

OUTSIDE THE THEATER

The IRS and Wall Street have tricked investors for years with reflections of wealth as opposed to the real deal. Society sees a guy in the spotlight with a mansion and a fleet of Italian sports cars, and everyone thinks that person is wealthy. In the second spotlight on the other side of the stage, we see a woman stepping off her yacht or exiting her personal jet, and we think that's a rich and successful person. We're constantly told that the way you know you've "arrived" is if you have many things that cost a lot of money. That is the clear signal to others that we've made it and have a lofty net worth.

Wealth, we are told, is the name of the game. But the truth is, it's just a reflection of the real objective. Behind the dark curtain is *income*—the genuine article. In our race to show off our wealth, we are more like a rat on a wheel consuming material goods while trying to keep up with the Jones family. Before I raise the lights and show all the mirrors involved in the difference between wealth and income, here is how most people get deceived by this powerful illusion.

THE REAL-LIFE PERFORMANCE— WHERE IS THE MONEY?

Tre and his wife, Kimberly, are both attorneys at a high-powered law firm downtown where they work long hours and focus intently on how much time they can spend billing clients. They each specialize in different areas of law and, now in their late thirties, are known throughout the firm as a power couple. They own a few expensive luxury cars and have a beautiful home that would be out of reach for most Americans. They tend to splurge on clothes, and they each have their own designer interests in their custom walk-in closets, including Italian shoes and the finest silk ties. They created an oasis in their backyard with a pool, complete with an outdoor kitchen and a gas-fed firepit. When you include their jewelry, their beach house, and the money in their retirement plans, any outsider would guess they are worth well over a million dollars.

Tre and Kimberly visit with their financial advisor and banker every year, because they are serious about growing their net worth. At one of those annual meetings, their banker compliments the power couple on their success, and he goes on to explain that now they can afford to buy a much bigger, bolder home. He says to them, "Throughout the years, my team here has always done a good job helping you to answer the question, 'Do you have enough money to make the purchase?' Now, I am pleased to tell you that you have enough money to take the next step and buy your dream home. How does that sound?"

After talking to the banker, Tre and Kimberly hire a real estate agent and begin searching for the home of their dreams. Soon, they find a true mansion that is simply impossible to resist, though it's a little bit outside their price range even with the attractive loan package the bank is offering. To help cover that extra cost, Tre and Kimberly approach their law firm to ask for an advance on their annual bonus, and it's in their bank by the end of the week. They make their offer on the house and soon are the proud owners of a new home in one of the wealthiest areas of town where they already have several acquaintances.

Now in a mansion that costs seven figures, the couple have dinner parties regularly for colleagues and clients. Their guests drive into the gated neighborhood and pass by the private country club. Everyone who walks through their front door comments on the brilliant chandelier and paintings in the foyer. Friends and clients alike can't help but admire the intricate crown molding on the ceiling above the 12-person dining room table.

Guests often leave Tre and Kimberly's house thinking about how they'd like to be successful and wealthy in the same way. Some might feel a little jealous at how Tre and Kimberly are handling their finances so well. But all of them, including Tre and Kimberly themselves, have been tricked, because it just takes one small step out of alignment with the proverbial mirrors for every reflection of wealth "owned" by the Jones family to disappear.

THE ALL-POWERFUL VIP PASS— REFLECTION VERSUS THE GENUINE ARTICLE IN REAL LIFE

What do you direct your hard-earned money to buy for you? Cars, designer clothes, electronics, fancy watches, yachts, airplanes, brand-name accessories, a mansion . . . and the trick is on you. Especially if you've ever said, "Use your money to make more money." The simplest way to turn up all the lights on Tre and Kimberly's illusion is to demonstrate where the mirrors are located, so that the reflections are obvious in comparison with the real thing.

To find the reflections in Tre and Kimberly's Hall of Mirrors, let's recall that when they used their bonus money to buy the big house, they made a trade just like any of us do whenever we buy something. If you walk into a store with $5 and buy a candy bar for exactly $5, you will walk out of the store with the same net worth. Before the trade, you held your value in dollars, and after the trade, you held the value in the form of candy. So is the $5 a reflection, or is the candy a reflection? Which is the genuine article? *Spoiler alert:* The $5 is not the real McCoy, and the reason you thought it was is proof of how common and deceptive this trick is.

Tre and Kimberly gave away liquid currency (some from their savings, some from the bank loan, and some from the advance on their bonus at work), and in exchange, they received a home. On paper, the value of their assets at that moment was unchanged because they'd changed the funds into a house with windows, doors, and fancy chandeliers (not to mention a loan as well). So to find the mirrors in this situation, our question is, "Between the cash bonus from the law firm and the mansion itself, which is a reflection, and which is the genuine article?"

Remembering that a reflection cannot exist without the genuine article, most people would say the house is a reflection, and that's correct (but it's only part of the answer). It should be obvious that owning a home costs money. As soon as Tre and Kimberly make the trade and purchase the house, their lifestyle—their need to create income—just became bigger. The mansion requires maintenance, insurance, repairs, property taxes, and, in this case, interest cost on the loan. This means that the house isn't just a reflection; it's like a thirsty vampire that Tre and Kimberly have invited into their lives to feed on their finances. As soon as there's no money available, the reflection of the vampire home disappears, because the bills have gone unpaid, the utilities have been turned off, and the government wants its back taxes that are long overdue.

Many people think that the loans are the problem with this scenario, but that's not accurate. If Tre and Kimberly can't afford to maintain the home, then they will lose it, and that is true whether they took out a loan or not. The interest on the loan is just one of many ways the home continues to require funding. Debt just adds to the myriad of extra costs when we acquire reflections of wealth that need money to maintain their existence. Debt itself is not the main issue, but it does compound it.

Another aspect of this illusion that easily tricks people is that when they guess the house is the reflection, they miss the fact that the saved-up bonus money is a reflection as well. Almost no one realizes that *both* the cash bonus and the home are reflections at each side of the stage because they both are dependent on something else to survive. In one spotlight on the right, the house needs funding for a variety of things, and in the spotlight on the left, their bonus and other earnings from the law firm exist by virtue of the couple's daily effort and success at work.

Both the cash bonus and the mansion are dependent on something else to exist. The extra money wouldn't exist if it weren't for Tre and Kimberly using their minds and bodies to go out and make income. They are standing in the middle of the stage behind the curtain, and if they move (make a change), their reflections of wealth vanish.

WHAT TO DO: AVOID THE SYSTEM, AVOID THE PROBLEMS

Like many of you reading this book, Tre and Kimberly themselves are the only genuine article in the situation. As soon as one or both of them make a change (stepping out of line with the mirrors), their income ceases, and neither of their reflections—not their bonuses from the law firm or the mansion—can continue to exist in their lives. The only way the home gets purchased is if they have the money in the bank to afford it, so the home is a reflection dependent on that advance bonus. The only way the money exists in the bank is because of their work and reputation at the law firm, so the pot of money in the savings account is a reflection dependent on Tre and Kimberly themselves.

ACTION STEP: Don't just look at the cost
of buying something. Instead, look at
the cost of buying and maintaining it.

When I was growing up, my mother used to say to me, "Of course
you *can*, but the question is whether you *should*." Wall Street's bankers
will always show their customers what they *can* borrow. But we all
know that just because you *can* buy something, it doesn't mean you
should. While this is an excellent bit of old-world wisdom, this advice,
unfortunately, is woefully incomplete.

How do you tell the difference between *can* and *should*?
Understanding the difference between income (the genuine article)
and wealth (the reflection) is a great first step. If you have set your
lifestyle (as described in Chapter 1) and saved up a pot of money, then
you *can* buy a fancy car. It doesn't mean you *should*.

Homes, and other purchases like them, supposedly prove to our
community that we have money, but many times these purchases
are just signaling to others that we *used* to have money. A yacht, a
fancy watch, a luxury car, a designer tie—they all have something in
common because they are all dependent on income to allow them to
exist (the tie must be laundered, the watch needs repairs, etc.). What's
worse, the more luxurious the purchase, the more it is just a vampiric
reflection creating a need for more income. Anything that is taxed
by the government, like a house or car, will forever require income
to keep it in your life. This means that when we dream of living in a
fancy mansion with chandeliers, we're really yearning to fill our life
with additional cost and financial burden.

When lotto winners and celebrities use their newfound wealth to
buy vampiric reflections that show the world how much money they
used to have, they are faced with feeding money to all those possessions. The downward cycle begins, and the more things they buy, the
faster those reflections of wealth use up actual money. Pretty soon, the
money is all gone.

The cost of keeping it is far more important to consider than *the
cost of acquiring it*. Because Tre and Kimberly are making the money

to cover the ongoing cost of the home, they must keep working to create income for as long as they own that mansion. That's how people get chained to work and suffer in the rat race. They're stuck! Now they must get up early every day and stay in line with the mirrors so that the images of wealth can continue to exist. It's the exact opposite of financial freedom. They don't own their possessions. In the Hall of Mirrors, their possessions own them.

Nevertheless, people want to own things. They approach their bankers, mortgage lenders, and financial advisors all the time to discuss large purchases. Wall Street makes sure to direct the conversation so that the public focuses on the question Tre and Kimberly's banker focused on: "Do you have the money to buy the home?" This is Wall Street's setup for the illusion. The phrase "to buy" and the question "Do you have the money" combine powerfully to trick the public into being consumers who are stuck in the rat race trying to create more and more income.

That phrase "to buy" is hiding something very important. Everyone has heard the saying, "Easy come, easy go." Lotto winners, athletes, and celebrities are famously rich one day and completely broke the next day. How could that happen? Wall Street and its financial experts should be helping people to properly ask the question, "Do you have the money to buy *and maintain* this purchase?"

The second, trickier part of this illusion is in the question, "Do you have the money?" This puts an emphasis on the banker's customers using up their hard-won earnings for the purchase. We're trained to save our dollars and then use those dollars to make a trade for something we want. That's what Tre and Kimberly did when they took their bonus and spent it on a house.

Wall Street shouldn't ask, "Do you have the money?" Instead, financial advisors should ask, "Does *your portfolio have the income* to support buying and maintaining this purchase?" They don't ask that because the Money Magicians want the public to think, "Money is money. I have enough to cover the purchase price, so I'm buying it." This is the epitome of a consumer mentality (and all money is *not* the same, and Wall Street hides this in other ways, which is discussed in the next chapter). When people fall for this powerful Wall Street trick, they continually spend their hard-won, personally earned savings on things that increase their lifestyle and bring them more financial burden. It's the formula for consumerism and the very definition of being stuck in the grind. It's also the opposite of growing your net worth and financial security.

ACTION STEP: Use your hard-won income to create ongoing cash flow that requires minimal to no effort from you.

In addition to the bonus from work, Tre and Kimberly pulled from their savings to buy their mansion, and those funds are a special kind of reflection. A pot of money or a savings account typically doesn't cost much in order to continue to exist, which makes it different from a car or boat. The hard-won earnings that Tre and Kimberly set aside are the principal that results from their labor. What makes principal so special? And what should we use that money for, if not fancy cars and big houses?

What makes our principal special is that it is the result of our dedicated, hard work. That means the money we make with our time and effort is different from the money we make because of owning things that pay us income. Money made by our own effort is limited by how much time, energy, and attention we can give to a task along with what other people will pay for us to do that task. Making money in this first-hand fashion is hard on us because we must stay in place in the Hall of Mirrors and run our own personal rat race. On the other hand, the money we could make by owning income-producing assets is nearly limitless. Some people call this "mailbox money" or "passive income."

As mentioned already, just because you *can* buy something doesn't make it a great idea. So when you have extra funds, what *should* you buy? Our principal—the money we earn from our own labor—is our *potential*. It's a means to an end, and we each get to decide what ends we wish to create. Everybody's pot of money has the potential to create something, and this potential is only bounded by our own minds. Wealth, therefore, is not "possession" of money or the various things it can buy. Instead, true wealth is utilizing—to the fullest—every drop of potential that your money provides.

Sadly, most investors and savers choose to *create* nothing. Instead, they consume other people's creations (cars, cigars, jewelry) in an effort to show their community that they are wealthy. But ironically, they only display proof that they no longer have that money.

How can we utilize the potential of our wealth? One person might want yachts and art, whereas someone else might use his hard-won principal to do science experiments over and over, thousands of times, until he finally creates a lightbulb that needs no electricity. Another person might use her savings to go to school and get more education, which allows her to earn a bigger wage. We each have our own dreams, and the potential of our money is, at the very least, an opportunity to achieve them.

There's an infinity of ways to use your money, but if you begin with the end in mind, the smartest choice is to turn your hard-won savings into an income creator. When you do this, you do some magic of your own! Once your savings are creating income for you, you've transformed that money into a genuine article. It's no longer a reflection.

Now, you have two sources of income: First is your own two hands as you deploy your time and energy in your career, and second is the income-creating engine you just purchased with your hard-won savings. Taking this step permits you to begin to face the scary truth that you might not be able to work forever even if you wanted to. Just like the magician who has to go to the bathroom, most people will need to step out of the Hall of Mirrors at some point in the future.

If Tre and Kimberly decided not to buy the mansion and, instead, used their hard-won principal to buy something that makes them income, what would they buy? A great path available to them (and to all of us) includes strategies such as dividend-paying stocks, oil partnerships, and real estate investment trusts. Much has been written on each of these, and there's a lot of potential income to be made in all three. The thing they have in common is that there's very little effort required on the investor's part to collect income from these sources.

But if Tre and Kimberly were open to doing a bit more work, they might buy things such as the following: a franchise; a rental home; or any number of home-based or web-based businesses. Either way, people have a lot of options to learn more if they are interested in exploring ways to turn their principal into an income-creating machine. Certainly, you can speak with your financial advisor, but you can also get a lot of great articles from a simple Google search under the heading, "ways to make passive income." Additionally, here's a short list of other resources you might consider:

- *The Mr. Money Mustache*, a blog by Pete Adeney

- The book *Choose FI: Your Blueprint to Financial Independence* by Chris Mamula, Brad Barrett, and Jonathan Mendonsa

- *The Financial Samurai*, a blog by Sam Dogen

- The book *Playing with Fire* by Scott Rieckens

- *Traveling Wallet*, a blog by Melissa Neacato

- The book *The Simple Path to Wealth: Your Road Map to Financial Independence and a Rich, Free Life* by J. L. Collins

- *2 Frugal Dudes*, a podcast by Kevin Griffin and Sean Merron

- *Our Next Life*, a blog by Tanja Hester

By investing their savings in the income-producing ideas that seem right to them, Tre and Kimberly could turn their labor (which resulted in money) into a self-sustaining genuine article. This would be the complete opposite of a vampiric reflection sucking dollars from their wallet. The income-creating machine adds money and security to their life and gets them closer to financial freedom.

If you keep your lifestyle fixed well below your wages, then some-day your saved money could create more income than you make with your two hands at work. At that moment, you are free to step away from the mirrors because your investments will continue to pay you. The key to this is living within your means and keeping your costs under control as described in the first chapter of this book. But what about those of us who would like to increase our lifestyle and live "the good life?"

ACTION STEP: When your passive income surpasses your active income, you can begin to consider increasing your lifestyle. The things you own should pay for the things you consume and enjoy.

The old story about the goose that lays golden eggs is a wonderful fable to drive home the point that people get easily distracted into believing that they want as much wealth as possible. But really, we need the income. When the villagers in the tale kill the goose, they destroy the very thing that makes the income possible. This is what people do every time they spend their hard-won principal on something that doesn't make them more income. Our savings accounts are like little magic geese that could each lay golden eggs, but instead, people kill their goose every month and spend the money on something that makes their life more expensive.

That leads us to a rule of thumb you'll never hear on Wall Street: *Don't increase your lifestyle until your passive income surpasses your active income.* You'll know you *can* and *should* buy that luxury item when the *cost of keeping it* is totally covered by your passive income. The things you own (such as dividend-paying stocks, oil partnerships, and real estate investment trusts) should pay for the things you enjoy and consume.

"Whoever dies with the most toys wins" is quintessential Wall Street. But that illusion serves only to distract people from the real race: Create and increase income. This is the only race that matters, and it's simple to win it! Let your investments provide the income needed to cover the cost of buying and maintaining the things that raise your standard of living. If you must use the money that you yourself created to make a luxurious purchase, then you shouldn't be buying that luxury item just yet.

The patience needed to do this can be very hard. Waiting may be simple, but that doesn't make it easy. For those who can delay instant gratification, financial freedom will occur when their passive income from investments covers the cost of their everyday lives as well as the luxuries they've been dreaming about. It's not wrong to buy an enormous TV or a fancy car or a yacht. You just shouldn't buy them with your hard-won principal. It's equally bad to use your personal earnings to cover the costs of maintaining your possessions after you make a big purchase.

ACTION STEP: Treat debt the same as a really sharp sword. Use debt sparingly for well-thought-out reasons. Maintain debt properly. Aim to retire your debts at a reasonable point in the future.

Everyone reading this book can imagine someone like Tre and Kimberly. Their chandeliers and fancy cars tell the world they are successful. But it's harder to clearly imagine how much debt Tre and Kimberly must carry with them everywhere they go. People rarely discuss how almost every dollar Tre and Kimberly earn at work goes into maintaining all those reflections of wealth. And no one wants to think about how easily Tre and Kimberly could lose everything.

There are any number of normal, everyday things that could destroy their various reflections of wealth. Insurance agents know this better than anyone else because they make a living asking us to take a moment and face the reality that bad things can, and often do, happen. It's reasonable to say that at some point, Tre and/or Kimberly might be injured or get too sick to continue working. In today's politically charged environment, either of them could say or do something on social media that reflects poorly on the firm, and they lose their jobs. Old age, both simple and inevitable, could force them into a different lifestyle later in life. And we've not even touched on divorce, theft, lawsuits, natural disasters, or the bank getting into trouble and calling their loans.

In the investment world, debt helps create transactions, trades, and purchases because the exchange couldn't have occurred without the extra money loaned to the buyer. Anything that is purchased with debt is more expensive than it otherwise would be because of the interest costs. If this purchase is something the buyer hopes to sell later for a gain, then debt and the interest payments slowly make it harder and harder to turn a profit as the weeks turn into years. Everyone reading this book has heard about the bank taking over assets because the loan wasn't maintained properly. Sometimes, the only way to service the loan is to sell the asset itself, and usually, when you're forced to sell, the price you get won't be a good one.

Debt is a lot like a sword in that it can win you a battle, but it also can cut off your own hand. Debt can speed you toward a greater profit, but it also can land you in bankruptcy. Debt itself, like a sword, is not evil. But it needs to be handled responsibly and always with an eye toward permanently retiring it someday.

ACTION STEP: Track the income your investments create with a projected cash flow report at every annual review that your financial advisor provides.

With your new income-focused mindset, you'll be more intent on increasing the potential for passive income, instead of just making more money to pay debt. What's more, you'll naturally wish to change the way you review your investment portfolio. Looking at how much income the account creates for you is very different from the typical focus on the amount of money you will have in the future. Luckily, your financial advisor can help you see the income predicted to be paid out, and it's very simple and convenient. In fact, the best investment advisors will provide their clients with a projected cash flow report (PCFR) that gives an income-oriented view of all the investments in the portfolio. For an example of one, feel free to email me at cmanske@manskewealth.com with the subject: "Requesting Example of PCFR."

This could be the most important information Wall Street shares with clients during an annual review meeting. Yet more often than not, most clients see only projections of the amount of money they will have in the future instead of the amount of income the account will create for them. Wall Street wants us focused more on the value of our holdings instead of the income those holdings are creating for us. Over the last 20 years, I've been shocked over and over at how often new clients tell me that their previous investment firm never provided a projected cash flow report, and they didn't even know what it was.

The projected cash flow report should list out every single invest-ment that an individual owns across all the person's various accounts. For each holding, the report should provide data to describe when, in the next 12 months, each investment pays out income and how much income will be paid. This allows investors to easily see that one investment might pay $100 next June, while another one might pay $25 every month.

An optimized projected cash flow report will display a total of all the income created by a client's portfolio on both a monthly and yearly basis. This allows investors to look ahead to a specific month and see the total amount of income that is expected to come in during those four weeks. It also clearly denotes the total amount of income for the entire 12 months, which is a great way to look at the annual "salary" created by the entire group of investments. The projected cash flow report is the picture of an investor's principal doing all the work of creating income while the investor herself is free to do other things with her time.

The projected cash flow report answers the question, "How much income will this produce for me next year?" and helps people rec-ognize their investment portfolio as a valuable, income-producing machine. Regularly examining this report can help create a mindset that has some beneficial side effects of its own. For one, it's a lot harder to panic and sell your income-producing machine when the market drops because it's clearer to you that each investment is doing something for you. It's paying you a nice stream of income that you could be using for something meaningful in your life.

It's also harder to panic and sell in the next bear market because this income-focused mindset completely reverses the "fear of missing out" that drives people to sell. Normally, FOMO and Wall Street's focus on "what's it worth" have people glued to how much an investment drops in value. They feel scared of losing more money, which creates panic and sometimes encourages poor decisions. Income-focused investors feel FOMO as well, but they are scared of losing the income that their investment creates. That means their fear and panic help them to hold on to their investments, because the easiest, quickest way to lose that income is to sell the holding that is creating it.

When my clients look at their investments this way, I've found they treat their portfolio a bit more like their home. If someone knocked on your door today and said he'd buy your home for half of what you paid for it, you would not seriously entertain the offer. Even if someone different came by every day for three months making abysmal offers while claiming your home isn't worth much, you'd just stay put. Of course, you'd worry about what was going on to affect the home price so badly, but your life would be fundamentally unchanged.

The main reason you wouldn't sell your home is because you know it is doing something valuable for you. It is keeping the rain off your head. Your fear of being out in the cold is greater than your fear of the house being worth less money. When the stock market falls in the next bear market and everyone is saying your portfolio isn't worth much, it's a lot easier to avoid selling in a panic when you can clearly see that the portfolio is keeping the rain off your head. It's creating income on a monthly basis. In fact, during those down markets you could choose to direct all that income to go right back in to buy more of those income-producing investments. In that case, you'd probably see, in your next annual review, that there's been a large increase in the amount of income that your investment machine is producing.

That's a successful way to buy low, and it's an added benefit that none of your own, personally earned dollars were needed.

ACTION STEP: Don't buy to sell; buy to earn!

Another beneficial side effect of paying attention to the income produced by your principal is that it encourages a less risky approach to buying investments in the first place. Most people will buy a stock or other investment with the hope that, later on, someone else will be willing to pay a lot more to buy it from them. This can happen—people do make profits at growth investing. But it carries more uncertainty than buying an investment that also pays income while the owner looks to sell it.

The race for wealth is fueled by the Money Magicians and their siren songs about the quick riches made by doing transactions. Wall Street loves to say, "Buy low, sell high!" and "Use your money to make more money!" But be very wary of this, because usually what's being sold is the hope that someone else will pay more to buy this very same thing you are buying. You must ask yourself, "Why would the next person want to pay more money than I did to buy the exact same thing?" You have probably heard the following quotes before:

"My cousin knows the guy who set this growth fund up. It's going to go through the roof!"

"Here's an amazing stock. The story is so compelling. Get in before it goes up!"

"Inflation's high, so buy these gold and silver coins. Later, collectors will want them!"

"My friend is selling his comic books and baseball cards cheap! You want his number?"

"Bitcoin is where everyone's making a killing! How are you not in that yet?"

In all those examples, investors won't receive any income. There's basically only one way they can make money with purchases like this. They must somehow convince someone else to buy that investment from them for more than what they paid for it a short while ago.

A great way to increase the odds that you are truly going to make money is to put a lot of energy and attention on getting an extremely low purchase price. You could also ask questions like:

"What will have changed to make someone want to buy it from me at a more expensive price?"

"What will be different about this investment or the investing environment so somebody else will want to spend more than I did?"

"Why haven't these changes and differences already occurred?"

"If I'm so confident I can sell this later for a higher price, why wouldn't the current seller just wait and sell it then?"

Do people sell things for more than what it cost them and walk away with a profit? Of course! It happens every day. But it's important to understand that in most cases, time is not on your side when you need to sell to make a profit. Maybe the asset is not vampirically sucking money from you until you sell it, but it's definitely taking up space in your life while keeping your funds locked away from other opportunities. Why not put time on your side? Use your money to make more income! Otherwise, you're just doing a transaction, and both the IRS and Wall Street love to collect, respectively, the taxes and fees on those transactions.

———

Your hard-won earnings depend on you to direct them. They have the potential to last your entire life and your children's children's lives if you choose to buy things that transform your principal from a reflection of wealth into an income creator. You can trade your wages for jewelry and a home theater system, or you can use your wages to purchase something that creates income. Do you want to kill the goose and turn all that income-creating potential into speakers and a flat screen? Or do you want to take care of the goose and collect its golden eggs over and over for multiple generations?

Certainly, you *can* buy the jewelry right now with the fruits of your own labor. But security and real long-lasting wealth come to those who plant the seeds of their hard-won earnings into fertile, income-creating earth. With diligence, your money tree will grow, and each branch of investment will bear fruit of its own. I'm suggesting you *can and should* use the fruit from that tree—this is the passive income—*to buy and maintain* the jewelry, fancy cars, and whatever else makes your dreams come true.

I'm also suggesting that the way we measure the cost of something should change so we aren't measuring the purchase price alone. We all need to be more aware of the cost of maintaining our lifestyle. This alone will go a long way toward helping us avoid the consumerism coming out of Wall Street so that we own our stuff instead of our stuff owning us.

If the Money Magicians rarely provide a projected cash flow report, then what are they showing investors? The most common report is an illusion called "average annual return," because Wall Street wants us to stay focused on how much our investments went up or down and how much more or less wealth we have from the previous year. In the next chapter, I suggest you flip the script and demand your bankers answer the question, "How much income will my portfolio produce for me next year?" The more energy you and your advisors give to this question and to this concept, the less likely you'll be tricked by the horrible question, "Do I have the money to buy it?"

DISILLUSION

HERE'S HOW THE STAY-AT-HOME SPOUSE GETS TRICKED IN A DIVORCE

It's usually a very difficult time when a couple decides to pursue a divorce, but it can be particularly painful and fraught with fear for someone who chose to leave the workplace in order to concentrate on managing the household. For this domestic-focused person, income is the critical, missing piece to his or her financial picture, because even if the spouse goes back to work, he or she is dealing with the disadvantage of years (sometimes decades) without job experience. Unfortunately, though *income* is the spouse's primary need, it's often the *asset's value* that drives the divorce process and determines how to split everything the couple owns.

The most common first step that attorneys suggest to the stay-at-home spouse is to try to understand the current financial situation by taking a detailed inventory of assets and liabilities in order to figure out how much will be needed to be able to pay the bills. But an inventory of assets and liabilities is not income focused. For stay-at-home spouses to really understand their personal financials, they need to put their income front and center so that they cannot be tricked in the negotiation and upcoming split of assets. The illusion occurs because everyone in the process from the attorneys to the judges acts like all the assets should be split based on what they are worth. It's a particularly nasty deception because the stay-at-home spouse often values the stability of staying in the home where the couple already lives, especially if there are kids involved.

From this faulty perspective, people think it's acceptable to split things using their value. For example, if the stay-at-home spouse gets the house worth $500,000, then the working spouse gets the family's stocks worth $500,000. But the person staying at home was just tricked. The stocks pay out money, which means they are an income-producing asset. Let's say that in this case, the stocks pay out $15,000 a year in dividends. Contrast that with the house, which costs money. If it's a half-million-dollar home, it might cost $50,000 a year in maintenance, insurance, taxes, and debt service.

One asset is a reflection of wealth and drains the owner's resources, whereas the other asset adds to the owner's income. Ten years from now, the stock has produced $150,000 in spendable money, and the house has used up $500,000 in spendable money. These are very different assets, and if you're the spouse without income, don't fall for this trick!

In this example, the negotiation of the split could start with the stocks being valued at $650,000 ($500,000 value plus an expected $150,000 over 10 years) and the house is worth nothing ($500,000 value minus $500,000 in costs over 10 years). The cost to maintain the asset is far more important than the cost to buy (or split) the asset. If you want to keep anything that does not produce income (such as homes, cars, boats, jewelry, art), then include their estimated costs over the next 10 years so the negotiation isn't lopsided.

THE GUESS THE NUMBER TRICK

How Do You Measure Investment Performance?

The magician smiles as a spotlight illuminates him in the center of the stage. He spins around, flaring his cape, and as if from nowhere, he produces a small glass jar filled with coins. He says, "Let's play Guess the Number," and you realize you've seen variations of this game before. In the local diner, during Halloween, there is usually a jar labeled, "Guess how many candy corn," and at school, the same fund-raising game is played with gummy bears in a bowl. So this measuring trick is not new to you, though you never imagined it to be considered "magic."

And then the magician explains, "In the early days of the traveling carnival, the magicians didn't do sleight of hand or large-scale illusions. Instead, they created measuring tricks in which attendees would try to estimate the proper measurement of something that people see every day."

THE ONSTAGE PERFORMANCE—HOW DO YOU MEASURE THE MONEY?

The magician's petite assistant saunters onto the stage in a leotard with pictures of dollars and coins all over it. Her hair trails to her waist, and she's wearing knee-high, platform boots with heels. She walks slowly and methodically to finally stand by the magician at center stage. He passes her the small jar of coins, which she holds with both hands.

He entreats the audience, "I won't ask you to guess how many coins are in the jar; it's clearly a small jar with a small number of coins. Instead, how much do you think the jar of money weighs? Even more fun, try to guess what the lovely Nancy weighs while holding this jar. Guess her weight—just call it out." People in the audience start yelling out numbers, and it's clear that most people are guessing she and the jar together weigh around 120 pounds. "My dear Nancy, is it fair to say that you weigh less than 120 pounds?"

"I'll never tell," the slender woman exclaims mischievously.

"That's OK, because we have a scale to tell us." Two other assistants roll out a comically tall scale. "Our audience says that you and that jar of coins weigh 120 pounds. Please step on the scale."

Nancy stands on the scale, and it reads 220. The audience gasps, because there's no way she is that heavy. Someone behind you calls out, "That scale doesn't work!"

The magician nods, clearly expecting the comment. He calls for volunteers from the audience, and three different people come up, and each tries out the scale. They all confirm that the scale works normally, and then they stand off to the side as Nancy returns to the scale. Stepping slowly and methodically, Nancy gets back on the scale holding the jar of coins, and it shows the same impossibly high number. You hear a woman in the audience to your left murmur, "How can that be?"

Suddenly, there's a shout from the back of the theater. "I know!" Everyone, including you, turns to see who is talking. A teenager calls out, "It's magnets! You have magnets inside the scale pulling down the weight of the coins."

The magician feigns a wounded look and says to one of the three audience members still standing on the stage, "Could you help me? I'd like you to try to pick me up. Just wrap your arms around me and pick me up. I weigh about 160 pounds, so the audience can see what that is like. Clearly, I am much bigger than Nancy."

The volunteer wraps his arms around the magician and lifts him up in a kind of bear hug. The audience applauds as the magician's feet come off the ground. Then, the volunteer walks over to Nancy, and she motions to go ahead and do the same thing. But when he goes to lift her, it's clear he's struggling a lot and she barely budges. The entire audience is stunned. Somehow, with that little jar of money, this tiny woman in just a leotard weighs over 200 pounds! It's magic!

THE ALL-POWERFUL VIP PASS— EASY VERSUS ACCURATE MEASUREMENTS ON STAGE

With your VIP pass, you walk up on stage and ask the magician the question that's on everyone's mind. "How does this work? You are fooling all of us, and we can't figure out how you are doing it."

The magician nods to Nancy, and she bends over at the waist to unzip her boots. As she steps out of them, the magician looks at you and says, "That's very special footwear, indeed. Platform boots with high heels look theatrical, but they also contain something very important. Go ahead and try to lift one of her boots."

You walk over and pick one up. The surprise shows on your face as you struggle to lift it. Nancy smiles and says, "The platform portion of the boot is solid lead. Each boot actually weighs 50 pounds. That's why I had to walk so deliberately. I've gotten some great leg muscles doing this job."

People use measurements to navigate through life all the time. In almost every situation, there's a quick and easy measurement available to us that, while inaccurate, is quite effective. It's usually pretty easy to look at someone and get a feeling for how much the person weighs. And even if we're a little off the mark, we are usually close enough that the guess is useful.

In a pickup game full of strangers, how do you know whom to select for your basketball team? Most people look to choose the taller people for their team. How do you know if your soup is too hot to taste? When we see the steam rising from the bowl, we might blow on it before risking a possible burn. More often than not, with a little common sense and observation, measuring the world around us seems pretty easy.

Measurements: Easy yet Imprecise Versus Difficult but Accurate

But it's important to distinguish that none of the above—height, temperature, weight—are accurate measurements. It can be quite hard to accurately measure things. For example, how do you hang a large picture frame in your living room so it's level? A lot of people just hang it on the nail and then adjust the picture by "eyeballing" it. Hanging a picture so that it is truly level and centered requires special tools and a time-intensive process. We similarly eyeball our surroundings to make "simple" measurements. We eyeball the height of strangers for our pickup basketball team, but properly assessing someone's ability at basketball would require a lot of observation of various skills. We could never tell the actual temperature of a bowl of soup just by looking at it.

OUTSIDE THE THEATER

Because these simple, commonsense approaches are often useful, we're fooled into thinking that all simple measurements are appropriate.

Occasionally, the "eyeball" approach to measurement is both imprecise and truly problematic, though we might not know that until it's too late. A perfect example of this used to occur when people used a paper map to choose a route for an important appointment. Today, real-time traffic data helps drivers reroute and avoid being stuck behind an accident. But years ago, someone would use a paper map to determine the proper route and the time needed to get there (usually by way of the shortest distance). The paper map isn't wrong; it's just an imprecise measurement of travel time. In the new world of GPS, we've come to learn that the shortest distance is not automatically the quickest travel time. This is why the satellite mapping services in modern cell phones are so special: They provide a measurement that is both easy (at least for the end user) *and* precise, which is a very rare and powerful thing.

Some Measurements Look Easy and Accurate, but Instead They Deceive and Misdirect

When I was a teenager, I did some competitive boxing, and I remember sparring with my high school best friend in his backyard. Whenever there was a good-sized group of guys over, my friend's dad would come out and coach us. He'd yell his favorite saying at us whenever we stumbled a little in one of these informal matches: "Did you put on your glove-sized shoes this morning?"

That was his way of saying we'd confused our glove size for our shoe size, and since we were wearing shoes that fit our hands, that's why we kept losing our footing. I share this because it is worth considering *why* it is such a ridiculous idea that somebody might actually wear shoes designed for their hands. There are two reasons: First, it's visually obvious, kind of like the "square peg in a round hole" exercise; and second, the bad results are easy to see and judge because such an error would be physically uncomfortable and possibly lead to serious injury.

But sometimes in life there are easy-to-make measurements that seem visually appropriate (square peg in a square hole), and their results are not as easy to judge. In these situations, the quick, simple measurement isn't just inaccurate; it's also deceptive. These are the dangerous moments when we make decisions that are not advantageous to us because we've done the measurement in a way that, while easy to perform, was inaccurate in a material way. Often, people will stand by their choices (based on easy yet faulty methods), and they're truly unaware of how different a path they'd have taken if only they'd made a proper measurement.

About 15 years ago, a friend of mine decided he was going to get back into the sport of boxing in his late thirties. I kidded with him that he was going through a phase trying to recapture his younger glory, and somehow I got hooked into helping him shop for his new gear. We went to the local discount store, walked over to the sporting goods aisle, and found all manner of baseballs, soccer balls, and lacrosse sticks. We also found a few shelves of boxing gloves. Each pair was clearly labeled in sizes small, medium, and large.

Naturally, we found someone who worked there and asked, "Where are the *real* boxing gloves?"

Size is not the proper way to measure a pair of boxing gloves. A boxing glove is measured by *weight*. People should want to know if they are attaching 12 ounces or 16 ounces at the end of each arm, because it's a very different thing to have to swing and hold up those different weights for extended periods of time. The impact is a lot different as well, because the more the glove weighs, the more padding there is to cushion the blow. But if you're new to boxing, you might not have a good frame of reference to understand the importance of that measurement. That makes the sizes—small, medium, and large—truly deceiving.

Talking with a couple of sales representatives that day, we learned that the vast majority of customers buying boxing gloves at that store were never going to participate in the sport of boxing. Mostly, they were doing fitness classes that required hitting a bag. The folks in the sports equipment industry decided to offer an easy, but inaccurate, way to measure the product. They found their target market would be more comfortable buying gloves with sizes that they recognized.

Therefore, in order to sell more boxing gloves, the manufacturers offered "small, medium, and large" as a measurement of the gloves instead of the more unfamiliar but accurate number of ounces.

Companies want to sell products, and they work hard to figure out what small changes could lead to big sales. From that point of view, it's not hard to understand why boxing glove manufacturers might give their product a label that doesn't work at all for the actual sport. It's the same thing as strapping on a pair of platform shoes that are made mostly of solid lead. When customers look at the shoes, they see something they understand, even though it's wrong. It's the difference between an easy assessment and an accurate one.

Wall Street benefits in a similar way when investors look at their portfolio the "easy way" instead of the "accurate way." The reported profit could be extremely different from the actual profit depending on the method of measurement. One of Wall Street's most common reporting methods is simple to understand but can cause real misdirection. Before I explain how this trick is performed and the reasons why, let's look at how people often discuss their portfolio performance in the real world.

THE REAL-LIFE PERFORMANCE—HOW DO YOU MEASURE THE MONEY?

It's a beautiful day on the pickleball court, and Alexia and Sarah have just enjoyed their weekly game that they've played together for almost 20 years now. In that time, the two friends have gotten close enough to talk about their money candidly with each other. As Sarah puts her gear into her bag, Alexia suggests they head over to the restaurant for some lunch.

On the way to the restaurant, Sarah asks, "Do you remember when we won that tournament together 12 years ago?"

Alexia nods. "How could I forget?" she said. "Two hundred thousand dollars! Split equally, that was a fantastic day, my friend. What made you think of that?"

"I met with my investment advisor recently, and I really wish you would have invested with my guy. The returns he's gotten for me have been phenomenal. Last time we talked about it, I think you said you were getting something like 6 percent on your money, right?"

"Yeah, good memory, Sarah. Look, almost every year now, you've told me your investments are doing better than mine. I just like my guy's approach, and I'm happy you have some profit."

Sarah snorts: "*Some* profit? Last year I got over 60 percent! And this year, it's like 25 percent."

Alexia can't help but think about how nice it would be to get such great numbers. "Well, maybe I *should* talk to your guy. I think you did something like 10 times better than me last year. And this year, I'm only making about 6 percent again."

"You definitely should talk to my guy, Alexia. I'm telling you, he's the best!"

Alexia frowns as they reach the restaurant door and then says, "All right, let me ask you something. We've both been investing with the same amount of money for the same amount of time. These last 12 years, my average annual return overall is 6 percent—what's yours?"

Sarah looks her in the eye and replies, "Mine is double that. No joke! My average annual return these last 12 years is about 12 percent. You can't be surprised, Alexia. Remember that first year? I told you I had over 60 percent profit and then the second year over 50 percent profit. I'm averaging something like 12 percent after all this time. And you've got 6? That's not good, my friend."

Alexia shakes her head as she opens the door for Sarah. Watching her walk into the restaurant ahead of her, she thinks, "Double my return!" Before they've reached their table, Alexia has decided to talk to Sarah's broker.

But she shouldn't talk to Sarah's broker. No one should change advisors or investment strategies with this information. As we pull back the curtain on this illusion, you will see that someone can have a 12 percent return *yet have less money* than someone with a

THE GUESS THE NUMBER TRICK

6 percent return. It all depends on how we eyeball the performance of our portfolios.

THE ALL-POWERFUL VIP PASS—
EASY VERSUS ACCURATE
MEASUREMENTS IN REAL LIFE

To explain how Wall Street often entices us to measure our portfolios, let's create a scenario with three different investors who each invest the same amount of money for the same amount of time. We'll call them Ben, Leo, and Luanna. They each invest their $100,000 very differently with the same broker, and after 12 years, they decide to openly compare notes.

The three of them go to the broker's office, and Ben speaks up first. He says to the broker, "We would like to know who has the biggest average return." Their advisor provides them those numbers in a single document, Table 3.1. The table gives performance figures for 12 years of investing. It also details what percentage of profit or loss each person earned along the way. The overall average for each person is listed with question marks.

After the three friends look over the table, the advisor says to them, "Let's play Guess the Number. Who do you think has the biggest average?"

They each take a few moments to really look at the table. Ben happens to be sharp with numbers, and he can calculate his own average in his head. It's easy, because he sees 11 percent and 9 percent repeatedly, and he knows that the average there is 10 percent. But it's a little harder to calculate the average for Leo and Luanna. Ben pulls out his phone so he can use a calculator to figure out the answer.

Table 3.1 Who Has the Biggest Average Return?

	Ben, $100,000.00	Leo, $100,000.00	Luanna, $100,000.00
Year 1	11%	10%	12%
Year 2	9%	20%	23%
Year 3	11%	30%	34%
Year 4	9%	−10%	15%
Year 5	11%	20%	−26%
Year 6	9%	5%	−37%
Year 7	11%	−5%	−18%
Year 8	9%	−15%	19%
Year 9	11%	20%	21%
Year 10	9%	20%	22%
Year 11	11%	30%	23%
Year 12	9%	−10%	34%
Average return	??	??	??

Before Ben finishes the calculation, their advisor hands them Table 3.2, which shows that they all have the same average. The three friends lean forward in their seats because none of them were expecting the three scenarios to have the exact same average annual return. After all, the numbers look really different. For example, Luanna had two years where she made 34 percent profit, and the other two don't seem to come close to that.

Luanna exclaims, "I was pretty sure I had the best average annual return." Leo and Ben agree that they expected the same. Learning otherwise indicates there may be more to this comparison than they originally thought.

Ben finishes with his calculator and agrees—they all have earned an average of 10 percent per year. He says to the broker, "So I guess that means we all have the same amount of money too. Can you explain better what we're looking at here?"

Table 3.2 They All Have the Same Average

	Ben, $100,000.00	Leo, $100,000.00	Luanna, $100,000.00
Year 1	11%	10%	12%
Year 2	9%	20%	23%
Year 3	11%	30%	34%
Year 4	9%	−10%	15%
Year 5	11%	20%	−26%
Year 6	9%	5%	−37%
Year 7	11%	−5%	−18%
Year 8	9%	−15%	19%
Year 9	11%	20%	21%
Year 10	9%	20%	22%
Year 11	11%	30%	23%
Year 12	9%	−10%	34%
Average return	10%	10%	10%

The advisor explains how the average annual return (or the "arithmetic mean," as it's formally known) is calculated. Almost everyone recognizes the formula of adding up all the performance figures and dividing by the number of years. It's an easy calculation to do, and most of us learned it in elementary school. As an example, if Frank reads 10 pages the first hour, 11 pages the second hour, and 12 pages the third hour, then to get the average pages per hour that Frank reads, we add 10 + 11 + 12 and divide by 3. A lot of people can do this in their head and quickly understand that Frank reads an average of 11 pages per hour. The arithmetic mean is the simple, regular way to examine data like this, and the majority of people can quickly understand it.

The friends take in this information, but Luanna can't stop thinking that there's something missing. She says, "I really believed I had more money than Ben and Leo. All these years, I've been talking about the big profits I've been making in comparison with them. And when I look at the table, I see bigger numbers in my column. Are you telling me I'm wrong about that? We all have the same amount?"

Leo responds to Luanna's question with a shrug, saying, "We started at the same time with the same amount of money. Now we know that all three of us achieved a 10 percent average annual return. Of course, we have the same amount of money."

Their advisor says, "I have another table to show you, and you're going to see that the three of you do *not* have the same amount of money."

Ben says, "I knew it! Luanna does have the most! But how does that work? If all of us have the same average annual return, why don't we have the same amount of money?"

The advisor replies, "I think you are in for another surprise, Ben," as he hands the trio of friends another document. It's Table 3.3, showing who has the most money. The friends look at that table in a way that people might puzzle over a slightly built magician's assistant somehow weighing over 200 pounds with just a small jar of coins in her hand. The normal, easy way of computing the answers didn't work.

Table 3.3 Who Has the Most Money?

		Ben, $100,000.00		Leo, $100,000.00		Luanna, $100,000.00
Year 1	11%	$111,000.00	10%	$110,000.00	12%	$112,000.00
Year 2	9%	$120,990.00	20%	$132,000.00	23%	$137,760.00
Year 3	11%	$134,298.90	30%	$171,600.00	34%	$184,598.40
Year 4	9%	$146,385.80	−10%	$154,440.00	15%	$212,288.16
Year 5	11%	$162,488.24	20%	$185,328.00	−26%	$157,093.24
Year 6	9%	$177,112.18	5%	$194,594.40	−37%	$98,968.74
Year 7	11%	$196,594.52	−5%	$184,864.68	−18%	$81,154.37
Year 8	9%	$214,288.03	−15%	$157,134.98	19%	$96,573.70
Year 9	11%	$237,859.71	20%	$188,561.97	21%	$116,854.17
Year 10	9%	$259,267.08	20%	$226,274.37	22%	$142,562.09
Year 11	11%	$287,786.46	30%	$294,156.68	23%	$175,351.37
Year 12	9%	$313,687.25	−10%	$264,741.01	34%	$234,970.84
Average return	10%		10%		10%	

First, they all had the same 10 percent average annual return, which didn't seem possible given the difference in percentage profit each year. Then, despite having the same average annual return, their portfolios have different amounts of money in them. But what really makes them scratch their heads is that *Luanna, who has the biggest percentage of profits each year, has the least amount of money.* How can this be?

How does Ben have the most money? Why do they have different amounts of money when their average annual return is the same? The answers lie in the difference between the easy measurement and the accurate one.

The arithmetic mean simply doesn't measure portfolio performance accurately. It's almost like using our shirt size to buy a pair of pants (or our glove size to buy a pair of shoes). Calculating profit over time requires different (and far more complicated) math than the elementary school average. The proper math is known as the "geometric mean."

The *geometric mean* is not something everyone learned in elementary school. In fact, it's quite complicated, and I've never met anyone who could do the calculation in his head. This formula requires that we multiply all the numbers in a given data set and then take the nth root for the obtained result. Here are the arithmetic mean and the geometric mean so that you can see the difference:

AM = (sum of observations) ÷ (total numbers of observations)

GM = $[(R1)\,(R2)\,(R3)\ldots(Rn)]^{1/n}$
where R = rate of return and n = number of values

As an example, Frank makes 10 percent on his investment the first year, 11 percent on his investment the second year, and 12 percent on his investment the third year. The first step in calculating the geometric mean is to multiply the three numbers, which looks like $10 \times 11 \times 12 = 1{,}320$. That's a simple first step (which can be hard to do mentally), and now it gets more difficult because the next step is to take the cube root of 1,320. A calculator tells us the answer is 10.969613104865. (For those that want to try this at home, just email me at cmanske@manskewealth.com, Subject: Geometric Mean Request, and I can share a step-by-step approach using a calculator.)

If we used the regular averaging approach (the arithmetic mean), we'd have gotten 11 as the answer. We can all agree there's not much of a difference between 11 and the geometric mean of 10.9696. It can often work out that there's not a big difference between the two measurements. But just like using your eyeball to hang up a picture frame, there's plenty of room for misunderstandings and inaccuracy.

Wall Street has something in common with the sporting goods manufacturers that sell boxing gloves in sizes small, medium, and large. Companies know that people are going to be more comfortable with the simple approach even if it's inaccurate. As long as the inaccuracy isn't horribly off-putting, the public prefers to do things the easy way. That means this average annual return calculation continues to persist right alongside small and medium boxing gloves or people eyeballing a picture frame. The easy way can be close, but it's not accurate.

For Ben, Leo, and Luanna, they had a hard time accepting that the average annual return doesn't accurately represent the actual dollars in one's pocket over time. They had to go back and look again at Table 3.3. Let's leave the three friends puzzled over this new reality and revisit our pickleball friends, Alexia and Sarah, so you can see just how misleading Sarah was when she described her portfolio.

The question was, "Should Alexia change to invest like Sarah?" Both started with $100,000, which they invested for 12 years. Alexia earned an annual average return of only 6 percent for that entire time, and Sarah earned almost double that. Alexia has heard Sarah over the years talking about how she more than doubled her money in the first two years. And just lately, the returns were 25 percent profit this year on top of 61 percent profit last year. We can picture this conversation happening because we all have that friend who loves to share her investment wins with everyone. It's normal for Alexia to feel a little envious because for years, she's listened to her friend mention in passing how she's made such big gains. But she's a loyal person who doesn't like taking risks, so she stayed with her financial advisor and the steady strategies for over a decade.

The fact is, the Alexias and Sarahs of the world believe that Sarah has more money than Alexia (just like Luanna thought she had more money than Ben). It's common to hear Wall Street say, "You must take some risk to make some money!" With that mindset, Alexia seems to be getting left behind, but Table 3.4 shows a very different reality.

Table 3.4 Slow and Steady Wins the Race

		Alexia, $100,000.00		Sarah, $100,000.00
Year 1	6%	$106,000.00	61%	$161,000.00
Year 2	6%	$112,360.00	59%	$255,990.00
Year 3	6%	$119,101.60	−10%	$230,391.00
Year 4	6%	$126,247.70	−38%	$142,842.42
Year 5	6%	$133,822.56	40%	$199,979.39
Year 6	6%	$141,851.91	−35%	$129,986.60
Year 7	6%	$150,363.03	−9%	$118,287.81
Year 8	6%	$159,384.81	30%	$153,774.15
Year 9	6%	$168,947.90	−11%	$136,858.99
Year 10	6%	$179,084.77	−31%	$94,432.71
Year 11	6%	$189,829.86	61%	$152,036.66
Year 12	6%	$201,219.65	25%	$190,045.82
Average return	6%		11.80%	

After looking over Table 3.4. it's clear that Alexia has more money. And that probably feels a lot like watching a slender woman step on a scale that says she weighs an impossibly large amount. Sarah has almost a 12 percent return, and Alexia has a 6 percent return, on average, for those 12 years. People think Sarah should have more money, but she doesn't because the average annual return doesn't accurately measure a portfolio's profit, just like our eyes don't accurately measure a person's weight. Both errors become clear with an accurate measurement. The mistake is laid bare when the magician's assistant steps on the scale or the two friends trade actual investment statements (which, as the Money Magicians count on, never happens).

WHAT TO DO: AVOID THE SYSTEM, AVOID THE PROBLEMS

Alexia has half the average annual return of Sarah, but she won the race. In fact, she has had more money than big-talking Sarah for the last five years! The dollars do not move in accordance with the arithmetic mean. The ripple effects from this improper measurement can be truly damaging as the Sarahs of the world keep investing in strategies that do not consistently grow their portfolio. For example, people might have great investments, but will do a lot of transactions to sell those positions because they think so poorly of their investment performance in comparison with their neighbors or what they are seeing on TV and social media. It's reasonable to suggest that individual investors are being tricked into selling good financial holdings, because transactions are the mechanism that unlocks taxes and fees, respectively, for the IRS and Wall Street.

And the average annual return isn't the only way our view of our profits gets distorted. "Change in value" is a data point that consistently trips up individual investors, and it's the main data point on the summary page of every investment statement you've ever received. The reason it is misleading is because people think that it represents profit, but it doesn't, and here's why.

In real life, investment portfolios can be more complex than our examples thus far for Alexia, Sarah, Ben, Leo, and Luanna. It's very rare for a portfolio to sit there for years with nothing coming in or going out, meaning it's normal that people are making deposits, borrowing funds from it, and doing withdrawals. Calculating your profit can get convoluted very quickly once you start adding in deposits and withdrawals. People complete deposits and withdrawals for a variety of reasons, which often makes it quite difficult for investors to accurately see how much profit they've made because all they see is the change in value on the statement showing if the account has more or less in it (and there's nothing in that change in value to indicate if it's profit or just your own deposits). In this way, change in value is even worse than average annual return!

The question is, "What is your profit as opposed to your own money that you deposited into the portfolio?" The change-in-value data point on your statement does not answer that question because it simply provides the difference between the account value in the past and what it is worth now. It is not a performance report at all because your deposits and withdrawals are treated the same as the profit from investment growth or dividends.

Here's why that's a problem. Take an account with $500 in it. Let's say you deposit $150 into that account. The next statement shows that the change in value is $150, and the account is now worth $650. It's increased by 30 percent! But it hasn't created a profit of 30 percent. Instead of showing you the account's profit or loss over time, you see a *change in value*, which is only helpful if you believe there's no difference between your principal and your profit.

We can all agree that a deposit of your hard-won earnings is not the same as the interest that was effortlessly added to your account simply because the investment distributed that interest income to you. How can we train ourselves to see our portfolio's profit more clearly? How can we avoid high-risk investments that post big numbers but actually lose money?

ACTION STEP: Look less at the size of the percentage numbers and more at the difference between them.

There are old stories and sayings that our grandparents used to share. One is "It's not the return *on* my principal as much as the return *of* my principal." And we all remember the story of the tortoise and the hare and accompanying wisdom like, "Slow and steady wins the race." But this isn't the focus anymore as people sprint to get ahead and constantly look for the big home run that will change their life.

Today, it's much more common to hear things like, "High risk, high return," while people keep spending their money on luxury cars and enormous homes. People believe they will somehow know when their high-risk investment will top out at its most valuable point. They *intend* to sell while it is high, but all the evidence points to the contrary. As discussed in the last chapter, individuals tend to buy high and sell low. How do we change this conversation?

Looking at the figures in all the tables in this chapter, you might notice a pattern: The investors with large downswings in their list of annual returns don't have as much money. The difference between the ups and downs, known as "volatility," is a killer of portfolio value. Lots of volatility is enticing if you have the secret to capturing only the upside, but in the real world, nobody knows how to honestly take risk and only win big home runs (if they did, they'd own an island somewhere). Losing money in a downturn is terribly hard on a portfolio's value, even though it's not so hard on the calculation of the average annual return. That's because the average annual return doesn't properly measure the change in dollars and cents over time.

For example, let's look at two basic scenarios. The first one is a positive 10 percent year followed by a negative 10 percent year. In this situation, our portfolio experienced a swing of 20 percent (the movement from positive 10 to negative 10). In a second scenario, we had a positive 5 percent year followed by a negative 5 percent year. For this second situation, the portfolio only moved a total of 10 percent (from positive 5 to negative 5). You, the reader, can pick whatever starting amount of money you wish to use because, over and over, the second example with less volatility will *always* have more money. Table 3.5 shows what that could look like.

Table 3.5 Lower Volatility Leads to More Money

Scenario 1 at $20	After positive 10%, it's $22. Then, after negative 10%, it's $19.80.
Scenario 2 at $20	After positive 5%, it's $21. Then, after negative 5%, it's $19.95.
Scenario A at $3,000	After positive 10%, it's $3,300. Then, after negative 10%, it's $2,970.
Scenario B at $3,000	After positive 5%, it's $3,150. Then, after negative 5%, it's $2,992.50.
Scenario Red at $400,000	After positive 10%, it's $440,000. Then, after negative 10%, it's $396,000.
Scenario Blue at $400,000	After positive 5%, it's $420,000. Then, after negative 5%, it's $399,000.

The Money Magicians hide another trick in all the scenarios above. If you calculate the average annual return of each scenario, you will *always* get zero. In each case, the average annual return suggests the investors break even, but you can see that in every scenario above, the person lost money! How can the person have lost money if the average annual return is zero? It's because—sorry if this is starting to sound like a broken record—the average annual return doesn't properly measure the change of the actual money in the portfolio.

Let's look at a simple example of how terribly powerful—and inaccurate—this illusion of average annual return can really be. If I have $1 and it goes down by 50 percent and then it goes up by 50 percent, the simple math says I've broken even. On average, 50 percent down and 50 percent up is zero. If I use elementary school math, my portfolio is supposedly unaffected and must still be worth $1 because that's what the arithmetic mean tells us. But from all you've read so far in this chapter, you know that this isn't accurate. In fact, it's almost the same thing as saying, "I have a gallon of money," or "Let me grab my glove-sized shoes." It's simply not the way to do the measurement.

Here's an accurate way to look at it. First, my dollar dropped by 50 percent, which means I'm left with 50 cents after that movement down. That means my pot of money is only worth 50 cents at the beginning of the next movement, which is an important fact to help pull back the curtain on this trick. The next thing to happen is the investment goes up 50 percent, which means I gained 50 percent of *50 cents*. That means it only goes up 25 cents. Therefore, if I start with a dollar, a drop of 50 percent and a gain of 50 percent leave me with only 75 cents! We're starting to see why our grandparents said, "It's not the return *on* my principal as much as the return *of* my principal."

When my investment went back up 50 *percent*, I didn't gain 50 *cents* to arrive back at one full dollar. In order to get back to my starting investment of $1, I needed to double my money. I needed 100 percent profit on my 50 cents. Instead, my $1 went down 50 percent to 50 cents and then went up 50 percent to only 75 cents. I've lost 25 percent of my money! That's a big difference from breaking even. It's important to be aware of the size of the swings in your investments.

ACTION STEP: Ask your financial advisor to provide an annual performance report that displays (1) starting and ending portfolio values and (2) a clear accounting of deposits and withdrawals.

The easiest solution to the problem of showing profit using average annual return is to look at your portfolio with a clear starting value and compare that with the ending value. Using the actual amount of money you had at the start in comparison with the amount of money you have now is an easy way to help make the performance report both simple and accurate, because you're measuring the change in the dollars instead of doing an average over time.

As an example, let's say Maria began investing with $1 five years ago. If today her investment is worth $2, then she made 100 percent profit over five years, which is about 20 percent per year. Pretty simple! Now let's look at this same situation with five years of data, shown in Table 3.6.

Table 3.6 Maria Makes $1 in Five Years

Year 1	$1 goes up to $7 = 700%
Year 2	$7 goes down to $6 = −14.3%
Year 3	$6 goes down to $5 = −16.7%
Year 4	$5 goes down to $4 = −20%
Year 5	$4 goes down to $2 = −50%

We know that Maria started with $1 and ended with $2. But if we were to calculate the average annual return, we'd need to add each year's percentage profit together and divide it by 5. It would show an average annual return of 119 percent in comparison with the more accurate 20 percent! If Maria were on the golf course or pickleball court, she might persuade people to do unnecessary transactions in their portfolios by bragging about her 119 percent growth.

Average annual return = [700 + (−14.3) + (−16.7) + (−20) + (−50)]/5

Average annual return = 599/5

Average annual return = 119.8%

Just as consumers gravitate toward easy-to-understand boxing glove sizes, the vast majority of people would be very happy when they're told that, after five years, their $1 investment had earned an average of 119 percent per year. Unfortunately, just because most people would love to see the bigger numbers the Money Magicians give them, that doesn't make it accurate. The proper way to calculate performance requires Wall Street to provide starting values (how much money on the day you opened the account) and ending values (the current value) in their performance reports.

Let's look at Maria's example again and just change one thing. She is going to save $1 per year and deposit it into her fund. This means she started with $1 five years ago, just like before, and the profit she makes over those five years doesn't change either because it is still exactly $1. That means she ends up with $2 for a 100 percent profit over five years.

Maria's extra money changes the scenario because the amount of money in her account has increased after she added more to it (so the addition is her principal, which is not to be confused with profit—more to come on that in Chapter 4). There is no extra profit in this second scenario for Maria since the only thing that changed is her annual deposit. She still just makes a profit of $1 over the five years. Table 3.7 shows what the account activity each year looks like:

Table 3.7 Maria Saves $1 per Year, but Still Makes $1 Profit in Five Years

Year 1	$1 goes up to $7 = 700%. Add in $1 at end of year to get $8.
Year 2	$8 goes down to $7 = −12.5%. Add in $1 at end of year to get $8.
Year 3	$8 goes down to $7 = −12.5%. Add in $1 at end of year to get $8.
Year 4	$8 goes down to $7 = −12.5%. Add in $1 at end of year to get $8.
Year 5	$8 goes down to $6 = −25%. Add in $1 at end of year to get $7.

Overall, Maria started with $1, put in $5, and earned $1 in profit. There is $7 now in the account. What does the inaccurate average annual return look like in this new scenario? You're familiar now with how it's calculated.

Average annual return = [700 + (−12.5) + (−12.5) + (−12.5) + (−25)]/5

Average annual return = 637.5/5

Average annual return = 127.5%

The deposits made the average annual return go up, even though the profit is exactly the same. In the first scenario, Maria earned an imprecise average annual return of 119 percent, and in the second scenario, it goes up to 127 percent even though nothing changed except she made some deposits. It cannot be overstated that the average annual return is only an illusion and cannot be used to help make serious investment decisions.

Continuing with Maria's example, if she looked on her monthly statement at the summary page, the change-in-value data point is just as misleading. Her change in value went from $1 to $7, so that looks like a 700 percent profit, or about 140 percent per year. I encourage all readers to take a moment and log into your online account and click on your monthly statement so you can see the document that your investment house publishes each month to describe your portfolio. You will likely see this change-in-value figure displayed as part of a summary of the account. It is incredibly misleading because all deposits are disguised to look like an increase in value (which benefits the Money Magicians because investors feel better when they can tell people they have seen their accounts grow over time). How can Wall Street get away with this?

It is not difficult for financial professionals to report their clients' gains clearly with deposits and withdrawals excluded from the profit figures. Every major brokerage firm has the software to create performance reports accurately. Table 3.8 is an example of a proper performance report (and we'll see it again in Chapter 4). The additions and withdrawals are clearly listed so that the client can be sure the reported returns are not being affected by money going in or out. Taxes will likely play a role in this, but for our purposes, if you wanted to see the total profit, you could add up the interest and dividend income along with realized and unrealized gains (which, for Table 3.8, is $865,731.87).

Table 3.8 can be easily provided by most financial advisors right now. The majority of firms use software that makes a table like this simple to create. Looking at it, how can you determine your profit? From 2014 to 2020, according to Table 3.8, the total additions over all seven years add up to $3,089,068.61, as seen at the bottom of the Additions column. That's what you deposited into the portfolio as your principal (congratulations on your success!). Since we know our profit over that time was $865,731.87 (by adding the interest, dividends, and gains), we can get a simple return percentage by putting the profit into your calculator and dividing it by all the additions:

Table 3.8 An Example of a Proper Performance Report

Time Period: 1/1/2014 to 12/31/2020

	Total Beginning Value	Additions	Withdrawls	Interest Income	Dividend Income	Period Realized Gains/Losses	Period Unrealized Gains/Losses	Total Ending Value	Return Percentage
1/1/2014 to 12/31/2014	$0.00	$2,939,068.61	$72,000.00	$19,808.78	$77,242.74	$13,118.27	$26,840.28	$3,004,078.68	4.56
1/1/2015 to 12/31/2015	$3,004,078.68	$0.00	$72,000.00	$17,206.54	$73,802.38	$22,180.76	$(181,034.85)	$2,864,233.51	-2.37
1/1/2016 to 12/31/2016	$2,864,233.51	$0.00	$72,000.00	$13,614.33	$83,012.96	$2,456.99	$181,968.55	$3,073,286.34	9.15
1/1/2017 to 12/31/2017	$3,073,286.34	$100,000.00	$72,000.00	$11,588.65	$92,810.56	$53,270.58	$82,392.96	$3,341,349.09	7.18
1/1/2018 to 12/31/2018	$3,341,249.09	$0.00	$72,000.00	$9,501.48	$95,321.10	$12,116.54	$(256,364.01)	$3,129,924.20	-4.45
1/1/2019 to 12/31/2019	$3,129,924.20	$0.00	$72,000.00	$9,627.61	$89,218.92	$40,176.49	$255,624.24	$3,452,571.46	11.43
1/1/2020 to 12/31/2020	$3,452,571.46	$50,000.00	$72,000.00	$7,756.01	$85,818.04	$22,707.69	$(96,052.72)	$3,450,800.48	0.59
Totals		$3,089,068.61	$504,000.00	$89,103.40	$597,226.70	$166,027.32	$13,374.45		

$865,000 divided by $3,000,000 is about 28 percent, which means you averaged about 4 percent per year. (If your reaction is, "Only 4 percent? That's terrible," then you might want to look at Alexia's and Sarah's investment reports. Slow and steady wins the race.)

My point is that none of this is reported on the typical brokerage statement, and the closest you can get to it usually is change in value. We all need to demand better so that we can see our money clearly. As it is, the Money Magicians ensure we continue to trip and fall in our glove-sized shoes, and we don't even know it.

ACTION STEP: Give just as much attention, if not more, to the change in income that your portfolio creates year over year rather than only focusing on the change in asset value.

In Chapter 2, I made the case for the importance of the projected cash flow report, which describes how much income your portfolio will create over the next 12 months. This report is rarely provided to clients, but it's even more rare to see the percent change in that income over time. While the value of the portfolio can go up or down (and that's where the Money Magicians direct all our attention), the amount of income your portfolio creates for you can also go up and down. Why doesn't Wall Street give an accounting of that?

For example, if last year my portfolio was worth $100,000 and this year it's worth $90,000, my financial advisor would be talking about the 10 percent drop and trying to explain what happened (and more than likely, most investors would only have eyes for that loss of $10,000). But how much income did my portfolio create last year in comparison with this year? It's rarely discussed. Did my income stay the same? How much did it change? What if last year I earned $400 a month and this year I earned $500 a month? As mentioned in the last chapter, if people focused more on the income their portfolio was providing them, they'd be less inclined to sell in fear because they wouldn't want to lose the interest and dividends that the holdings are paying them.

For a lot of people, there's a lightbulb that turns on as they get closer to retirement. These retirees think, "Why do I care what someone will pay me to buy my stocks and bonds? The current value is less important to me than knowing how much income the asset is paying me while I hold it." It's as if they turn a corner and suddenly realize that Wall Street would rather that people focus on what their assets are worth, so they will be more likely to buy and sell as those values go up and down. But the retirees want to give more attention to how much their assets pay them.

When this change in perspective happens to you, you'll find yourself thinking of your money like an apple tree that gives you all its fruit. That income—the fruit from the tree—is immediately useful, while the current value of the tree can only be realized if you sell the asset and give up all the future fruit it will provide. And when you sell the tree, that transaction probably creates fees for Wall Street and taxes for the IRS.

When people get a job, they tend to think about their work in terms of income. It's normal to ask, "How much do I earn, and how do I make more?" It's even more normal to examine the amount of the increase in income you make each year. "Last year, I earned $50,000 and I got a 10 percent raise, so now I earn $55,000." This is typical, and it should be the same for a portfolio, but the Money Magicians don't measure that for us because they want to keep us focused on how much the portfolio is worth. Without any report showing us the change in income over time, we see our investments in a way that makes volatile investments more attractive, and all of this leads to additional transactions.

Consider treating your money like a large apple orchard with a lot of space for trees. Each investment is a tree, and the dividends and interest are the apples that tree yields. Just like you try to get pay raises in your career, you want to increase the yield from your orchard. If your portfolio holdings are trees, then you can plant their fruit to create more trees, thereby increasing your investment holdings and the income you collect, because all the new trees provide you their apples as well. This is a powerful cycle that compounds over time.

You can pay closer attention to this by demanding that you get to see how much your investments are paying you and when they will get pay raises.

Maybe your investments used to make $1,000 a month and now you're up 50 percent, which means the investments pay you $1,500 a month. Of course, taxes will play a role in this, but that's still meaningful performance because real money is being created that is immediately available to you without selling the asset. The actual value of the investment creating that income might have gone up or down, depending on the year, but you only realize that profit or loss by doing a transaction, i.e., selling it off because you misunderstand it as an underperformer. That's precisely why the Money Magicians want to keep your eyes on the asset value instead of the asset's income. But what you see is not what you get.

If the portfolio pays a client enough to be comfortable in retirement and that interest and dividend stream isn't decreasing, then why would the client want to sell? But to know what's happening with the stream of income, we must require Wall Street to report to us both how much income we are receiving (using the projected cash flow report) and how that stream of income has changed over time. I suggest you give just as much attention, if not more, to the change in income that your portfolio creates rather than only focusing on the change in asset value.

Now that you know all about accurate and inaccurate measurements and how they are used by the Money Magicians, let's move beyond the math to examine the display of the numbers. In Chapter 4, we explore how Wall Street and the IRS display the individual position data in the statement (whether online or in the mail). That "data display"—investment name, number of shares, value per share, cost basis—can be very misleading and often causes people to sell good, profitable investments by using an illusion that makes the assets appear to be losing money.

DISILLUSION

HERE'S HOW THE HIGHLY PAID EXECUTIVE GETS TRICKED INTO KEEPING BAD INVESTMENTS

When a company's executive has a large salary and earns a lot of stock options or stock grants, the executive's pay and a lot of the executive's assets are tied up in one company. While there are many ways to address this imbalance of risk, one of the most common approaches is to offset the aggressive assets with lower-risk, conservative assets like bonds, especially municipal bonds. Whenever I review these portfolios and talk to executives about their bonds, they almost always mention something about the great yield, which is the income that the bond is paying them each year like interest earned in a savings account.

If an executive owns a local municipal bond, then all the interest that the bond pays her each year is completely tax free. For someone who makes a lot of money, tax-free income can be a compelling benefit. But whatever kind of bond she owns (corporate or government), the way the Money Magicians show her these investments on her statement is very sneaky—kind of like average annual return—because the Yield column appears to give a straightforward measurement of income. Unfortunately, there's more behind the curtain than people initially realize.

To see that clearly, we must understand that bonds are actually loans—and no one is going to loan out their money forever. When people buy a local county bond, they are loaning the county a certain amount of money (face value) and expect a certain payment of interest (the bond's coupon). Bondholders—people who buy bonds—want to get paid back the money they've loaned, so there's a point when the loan matures and the bondholder gets paid off.

The amount that the bondholder receives is what was originally listed on the bond, and this is not connected to how much the bondholder paid to purchase it.

In some market cycles, it's very common for investors to pay more for a bond than the face value, meaning they will get less than their purchase price back when the bond matures. For example, let's say the bond that the executive owns has a 4 percent coupon and is going to mature in three years. When the executive recently bought it, she paid $109, which was a bit more than the face value of $100. This bond pays out $4 a year (which is 4 percent of the original loan of $100), which means that while it's listed on her statement at a value of $109, her *yield* on the bond is listed on the statement as 3.6 percent. She looks at that and says, "I'm making 3.6 percent tax free, so it's almost the same as getting 5.5 percent a year that I'd have to pay taxes on. And since the bond has very little risk, I'm happy!"

But the problem is that she is guaranteed to lose $9 over the next three years because she paid $109 for a loan that, when it is paid back, only pays back $100. That means she's not really making 3.6 percent tax free (as listed on the statement), because the Money Magicians are ignoring the guaranteed loss of principal when the bond matures. What's actually happening each year is she's making $4 in interest and losing $3 in principal, so the yield should be listed as less than 1 percent. And because this new, more accurate yield is before any fees or charges that the Money Magicians might be collecting, the final, most accurate figure gets very close to zero percent.

Just like average annual return can be horribly misleading, the yield of a bond as reported on a brokerage statement does not give the full picture. When the statement says an investment worth $109 gives $4 per year that yields 3.6 percent, people think they understand what that calculation is saying because it seems straightforward. But the way the calculation is done makes it inaccurate. These inaccuracies make it harder for individuals to manage and control their finances because the data they are using to examine their investments is fundamentally flawed.

THE DISAPPEARING COINS ILLUSION

Are You Really Seeing Your Investments?

n the theater, the special medallion around your neck grants you ultimate authority over the magic show. An usher approaches to offer you some drinks from the menu, and as you order, a lot of activity is happening on the stage. Two magician's assistants bring out a small table with a black-and-red tablecloth. They set two large drinking glasses side by side on the table, both of which are half filled with various coins. It looks like a little kid emptied his piggy bank equally into the two glasses, and only had enough money to reach the midway mark. When your drink arrives, you signal to the magician that he's free to continue.

THE ONSTAGE PERFORMANCE— WHERE DID THE DEPOSIT GO?

"Are the glasses half empty or half full?" the magician asks mysteriously as he lifts one of the cups so you can see the coins moving slightly around inside. Then, when he knows he has the audience's attention, he slowly starts to pour that first cup of coins into the second one, dramatically raising his hand so the falling stream of pennies, nickels, and dimes gets taller and taller.

But wait! Where are the coins going? The cup on the table, also half full, doesn't alter in the slightest. The entire theater can hear the coins landing in the second cup, and yet it's not filling up. All the while the magician pours, the receiving cup looks unchanged with the same amount of coins only filling up the drinking glass halfway.

There must be a hole in the second cup. As if he could read your thoughts, the magician uses his other hand to pick the second cup up, and with the coins still pouring, you can see there's no hole. The coins from the first glass are simply disappearing into the second one. It's magic!

THE ALL-POWERFUL VIP PASS— ACTUAL MONEY VERSUS A PERCEPTION OF MONEY ON STAGE

You immediately wave your medallion to pause the show. When you reach the magician's table, you find an empty drinking glass sitting beside a second, similar glass that's half full of coins. Wondering how there were two cups half filled with coins but now only one cup is half filled, you pick up the second glass and see something you'd missed earlier.

There's a plastic film around the second, half-full drinking glass that has been printed with images of coins. It's a kind of costume for the cup that makes it appear half full of coins. No matter where you sit in the theater, that cup will always appear half full. It's not magic at all! The magician was simply pouring a half glass of coins into another empty glass that looked like it already had other coins inside. There was something physical between you and what you were observing, but you didn't know it. That thing—the wrapper with coin graphics inside the glass—manipulated your view so you thought you saw one thing when it was, in reality, altogether different.

OUTSIDE THE THEATER

A portfolio can only be "seen" as the data representing the holdings in each account, which means that your monthly investment statement is not actually your portfolio of stocks and bonds. Instead, the investment statement is more like the wrapper—the costume—around the glass that looks like money but is actually the thing between you and your money. Just like the costume on the magician's drinking glass, your monthly statement conveys information about what is inside your account.

There's data such as the number of shares, the market value of each position, the price you paid for each investment, and the yield or income you can expect to earn each year. This information is important because a group of investments isn't something people can touch or examine in the physical world. Instead, the statement is the lens that investors use to view and understand their finances. It is what's inserted between the observer and the observed, which, it's important to note, is not created by the investor. Both the statement and the data displayed online are gathered and formatted by the brokerage house holding your money, and the brokerage puts that statement together in accordance with IRS regulations. The layout of these statements, whether they're online or paper documents, offers the same basic information across the entire financial services industry, mainly due to strict regulatory oversight. (Since the data is basically the same on the paper statement as it is online, I'll just use the phrase "investment statement" going forward.)

The decisions that investors make about what is a wise or foolish move with their portfolios are often made based on what the Money Magicians display for you to see, instead of basic reality. In the case of the statement, the public often sees holdings that appear as though they should be sold when the reality is that they are perfectly good investments. The data in the monthly statement is a "wrapper on the glass," deceiving investors by standing between them and their money.

THE REAL-LIFE PERFORMANCE— WHERE DID THE DEPOSIT GO?

Sally comes home from work, checks the mail, and drops into a seat at the kitchen table. The first envelope she opens is the oversized one, her monthly investment statement. She often doesn't even look at it, but she was talking about her investments with some friends earlier, and it's on her mind. As she glances through her holdings—there are five of them—she sees that two look like they are losing money. She can tell because in the Gain/Loss column, the numbers are in parentheses. "The three other investments have gone up," she thinks, "so what's wrong with these two? Have they been down for a long time?" She quickly logs in on her cell phone, clicks on "Reports and Statements," and picks a statement from about a year ago. When it comes up, she can see those same two investments are showing a loss. And not a small one; she's lost thousands.

"This is crazy," she mutters to herself, and she calls her advisor, who happens to be her cousin Tony. She gets his voice mail at work, so she calls his cell phone, and when he answers, they make some quick pleasantries, and she realizes she's caught him at the golf course. She apologizes for interrupting and asks him when they can chat about her investments. He says he'll ring her back the next day.

When Tony calls her back the following day, Sally quickly grabs her statements and asks him if he could talk her through her investments. He pulls her account up on his system. He starts by explaining that, overall, she has five different investments. One is a technology stock, symbol TECH, and is a typical technology company. It doesn't pay any dividends, and after buying it about a month ago, it has gone up a bit. He sees on his screen that analysts expect that TECH will continue to go up in the same manner in the near future. Sally paid almost $10,000 for TECH, and she's happy with the profit she's made in the 30 days she's owned it.

The second of five investments is a growth-oriented mutual fund, symbol GFND, which has gone up so much that it's achieved thousands of dollars of profit in just a couple of years. Sally originally bought this growth fund for $16,000, and while owning it for two years, she's read a lot about how this fund manager keeps getting celebrated as one of the best minds on Wall Street.

The third investment, OLDX, is a stock Sally bought 10 years ago on automatic dividend reinvestment, and she can see on the statement that it's lost about $6,000. In fact, Tony reminds her he's told her several times that OLDX just keeps falling in price by about 50 cents per share every year in the last decade. OLDX pays the same amount of dividend dollars today that it paid out 10 years ago, and the news continues to report that since the income provided is not changing at all, OLDX's dividend isn't even keeping up with inflation. Tony tells her that OLDX will never be a "dividend aristocrat" since in order to earn the moniker, a company must increase its dividend every year for 25 years. Table 4.1 shows the statement data for the first three investments.

Table 4.1 Sally's Statement Data

Statement Data	Stock: TECH	Fund: GFND	Stock: OLDX
Quantity of shares	1,000.0000	1,000.0000	1,000.5101
Market price	$10.00	$20.00	$29.50
Market value	$10,000.00	$20,000.00	$29,515.05
Cost basis	$9,950.00	$16,000.00	$35,685.47
Unrealized gain/(loss)	$50.00	$4,000.00	($6,170.42)
Yield	n/a	0.22%	4.75%

"I've got two more investments, Tony. How about those?" Sally challenges, still reeling that she hadn't noticed the underperformance until now. The last two positions are stocks, symbols AAA and BBB, respectively, which Sally bought 10 years ago right around the same time as she bought OLDX. She remembers that she bought the same amount of AAA as BBB, and she asks Tony if he recalls what that original purchase price was. He says, "Sure! AAA was $30 a share when you bought it, and now it's $28. BBB cost $10 a share, and now it's $20. Wow, BBB has really been steadily going up, but AAA didn't change much up until about a year ago when it went down a bit." He also reminds her that since BBB kept going up, he sold a little bit of that position each year and used that profit to buy more AAA in a process called "rebalancing." Each year, he'd rebalance the two positions so they were equal in value again. Table 4.2 shows the data Sally and Tony are looking at during the conversation.

Table 4.2 Sally's Statement Data

Statement Data	Stock: AAA	Stock: BBB
Quantity of shares	443	621
Market price	$28.00	$20.00
Market value	$12,404.00	$12,420.00
Cost basis	$15,120.00	$6,210.00
Unrealized gain/(loss)	($2,716.00)	$6,210.00
Yield	1.17%	2.13%

Sally looks at the information on her monthly statement and says to Tony that she's trying to decide which holdings are the good ones as opposed to the ones that have not performed the way she'd prefer. "It looks to me," says Sally, "like OLDX and AAA are duds. They are down and have been down. They're not going anywhere or doing anything good for me. Should we sell them?"

"Well, you've held them for 10 years, and you have lost money," Tony replies. "I think I can find you something that will do better. Are you sure you want to sell them?"

"If I don't, I think I'll see that they've lost me money every month and I'll get stressed out. That's a glaring loss jumping out at me, Tony, every time I look at the unrealized gains and losses on the statement."

"I understand," Tony replies. "We can sell them both for a tax loss since they haven't really gone anywhere for a decade now. I'll put the sales in for you today."

And just like that, Sally and Tony have sold two of the best investments in her portfolio. They both were duped into thinking incredibly profitable investments had lost money because of the way the Money Magicians arrange statement data. The overall system tricked them into selling great investments by showing them the portfolio in a very deceiving way. Let's pull back the curtain on this common illusion where profitable investments are displayed as losers.

THE ALL-POWERFUL VIP PASS—ACTUAL MONEY VERSUS A PERCEPTION OF MONEY IN REAL LIFE

To best understand this illusion, it's helpful to leave the realm of finance completely, and for now, assume you are starting a farm that raises pigs. Let's pretend that all pigs, no matter what, cost $100 each. On day one, you buy your first pig for $100, and the next day, that pig has a litter of five piglets. That means that on day two, you have six pigs worth a total of $600, and all you paid for them is $100. On day three, you are feeling great, because you have a $500 profit on your original investment of $100.

Those baby pigs immediately grow up in our example, and they each have five of their own little pigs on day four. Your original cost for the 36 pigs on your farm is still $100 (leaving out food and other costs for simplicity). That means that on day five, you are really pleased to see that you've paid out $100 of your hard-earned money and you've made a profit of $3,500. Unfortunately, that night, the value of all pigs drops to $90 each, which means that the next day, things get very interesting.

A man with a Wall Street business card comes knocking on your door and says that he has a statement describing the financial situation for your pig farm. He hands you Table 4.3 and explains that with the drop in prices, your farm has a loss. Looking at the statement, you can see your operation has lost hundreds of dollars!

Table 4.3   Pig Farm Statement Data

Statement Data	Investment: Pigs
Quantity of shares (pigs)	36
Market price	$90.00
Market value	$3,240.00
Cost basis	$3,600.00
Unrealized gain/(loss)	($360.00)

What's happening here? You clearly made a profit with pigs, even if they dropped in value, because you only paid $100 to get the operation started. But the Money Magicians say you've got a loss of $360 because they don't report to you about your profit. Your statement does not tell you the gain or loss that *you've* made. Instead, the statement displays the gain or loss that *the IRS* will be levying taxes on. That is not the same thing.

The IRS treats our dividends, or in this case, your piglets, nearly the same as our hard-won income. You worked hard, saved $100, and used it to buy a pig. For you, the profit was over $3,000. But the IRS wants to get taxes on *everything you earn*, so it categorizes your baby pigs and your initial investment as almost the same thing. So the statement displays the data in a way that makes your hard-earned money that went in to buy the first pig look the same as the profit that you earned when the investment "birthed" a dividend, or gave more piglets.

Imagine that your farming experience didn't happen over a few days, but instead took a few years. For years now, you've been getting statements every month showing nothing about the real-life gain on the investment. Instead, that plastic costume around your portfolio has all been negative, statement after statement. What's more, let's pretend you never were on the farm itself and you never saw a single pig. The only view you've had all this time regarding this enterprise is the monthly statement from Wall Street. As time goes by, you keep examining your pig farm through the lens the Money Magicians have provided, and it's not hard to imagine that you'd be swayed to sell those pigs. No one likes losing money, and the reports clearly show your pigs are a losing investment.

So you sell the pig farm, lament the loss of $360, and decide to get into the business of growing roses. All rose bushes cost $1.99, so you buy one, and a year later, you take cuttings from that bush and plant five more bushes. At that point, you have six bushes for the original cost of $1.99 (keeping maintenance costs out of this for simplicity). If, in year two, you take five cuttings from all six of your bushes and plant these new cuttings, you'd have 36 bushes, and the original cost is still $1.99.

Let's say that, in year three, rose bushes go down in value and all the rose growers are worried that roses could go down 90 percent to just 20 cents a bush! What if the value dropped that far? You ask your advisor to show you an example monthly statement if the market for roses really did drop to just 20 cents per bush. He gives you the example shown in Table 4.4.

Table 4.4 Rose Bush Statement Data

Statement Data	Investment: Rose
Quantity of shares (bushes)	36
Market price	$0.20
Market value	$7.20
Cost basis	$71.64
Unrealized gain/(loss)	($64.44)

This is frightening to you, so you decide to sell all the rose bushes. But what the statement fails to show you is that even if the market dropped 90 percent, you'd have 36 rose bushes worth $7.20 and you only paid $1.99 out of your pocket for them. That's not the only thing missing. The Money Magicians also fail to show you that you could keep your rose bushes and take cuttings from them to plant more bushes. At 20 cents per cutting, you'd make more money keeping the investment than you would selling it. But the costume around your portfolio shows us a view of the investments that encourages us to sell, and this deception can be very hard to ignore.

The public often uses gain/loss data on the monthly statement to answer the questions, "What did I make?" and "How much did I lose?" Unfortunately, this data point does not answer those questions. Instead, it is like an IRS-required wrapper around a drinking glass tricking people into seeing an illusion of their investments. It's an incredibly powerful illusion because it influences us over time. Again and again, we see the loss listed every time we examine our portfolio. Even though it is inaccurate, it cannot help but affect our perception of our money.

Why isn't the reported gain/loss our actual profit or loss?

The typical statement uses a curtain of IRS tax rules to hide the actual profit created by dividends and rebalancing. Here's how those rules work on Wall Street if you buy 100 shares of stock in the fictional company, Simple Company. Let's say it's $10 a share, so the price is $1,000, and it pays you an annual dividend of a dollar per share. That means your holding in Simple Company pays you $100 per year.

After you choose to reinvest that dividend, the IRS will show that you paid $1,100 for Simple Company. But you didn't. You paid $1,000, and your stock had 100 piglets, which we call a dividend. That didn't change your original purchase price. A year later, those piglets grow up and have their own babies, which means the stock you purchased with the first year's dividend is now also paying you dividends. And your original purchase price still hasn't changed. You only paid $1,000 for it, but the IRS says all those dividends you used to buy more of the stock is the same as what you used to originally buy the stock.

If, after a couple of years, the stock declines by 10 percent, the Money Magicians show you that you've lost a lot of money, but you haven't. You bought 100 shares with your hard-earned savings, and then you used dividends to buy another 10 shares after the first year and another 11 shares after the second year. You now have 121 shares, and it cost you $1,000. If they are worth $9 a share now because they dropped 10 percent from the original $10 purchase price, your position is worth $1,089, which means you've still made money. But this is not what the monthly statement will display, as Table 4.5 shows.

Table 4.5 Simple Company Stock

Statement Data	Simple Company
Quantity of shares	121
Market price	$9.00
Market value	$1,089.00
Cost basis	$1,210.00
Unrealized gain/(loss)	($121.00)

The reality that is missing from the statement is that you have a profit of about 9 percent in Simple Company stock, and you can expect another increase in income because of buying more shares with the third year's dividend. Assuming all else is equal, Simple Company is looking great! But that isn't how the Money Magicians will show you this situation, because from their tax-centric point of view, you're down 10 percent.

Going back to Sally and her stock OLDX (Table 4.1), we saw that it had gone down in price each year for 10 years. The dividends received from the stock stayed the same each year and were reinvested. Her statement said she paid $35,685.47 for something that's worth $29,515.05, which means Sally lost $6,170.42. But in Table 4.6, you can see Sally's personal notes, which outline how she's actually doing as opposed to what Wall Street wants her to see. Note that if you add up the dividend dollars she received (it's in the second-to-last column), you get *almost $12,000 in dividend profit.*

Where is that profit listed on the statement? Are the Money Magicians hiding this information from us? Wall Street would say it is not hiding it; it is just reporting on the *taxable* gain or loss as opposed to the *actual* gain or loss. IRS rules muddy the waters, which

Table 4.6 Sally's Personal Notes on OLDX

Year	Purchase Price	Shares Owned	Market Value	Dividend per Share	Yield	Dollars Received	Shares Bought by Reinvesting
1	$35.00	687	$24,045.00	$1.40	4.00%	$961.80	27.4800
2	$34.50	714.4800	$24,649.56	$1.40	4.06%	$1,000.27	28.9934
3	$34.00	743.4734	$25,278.10	$1.40	4.12%	$1,040.86	30.6136
4	$33.50	774.0870	$25,931.91	$1.40	4.18%	$1,083.72	32.3499
5	$33.00	806.4369	$26,612.42	$1.40	4.24%	$1,129.01	34.2125
6	$32.50	840.6494	$27,321.10	$1.40	4.31%	$1,176.91	36.2126
7	$32.00	876.8620	$28,059.58	$1.40	4.38%	$1,227.61	38.3627
8	$31.50	915.2247	$28,829.58	$1.40	4.44%	$1,281.31	40.6767
9	$30.00	955.9013	$28,677.04	$1.40	4.67%	$1,338.26	44.6087
10	$29.50	1,000.5101	$29,515.05	$1.40	4.75%	$1,400.71	47.4818

THE DISAPPEARING COINS ILLUSION

means Sally's view of how much she paid for the stock has a wrapper around the glass. Sally—and the rest of us—cannot easily see that she has dividend profit, because those extra dollars are not displayed in a way that matches with our common sense of gain and loss.

If the statistics were displayed the way customers want to see them, then it wouldn't be so hard for both Sally and her financial advisor to see that the true purchase price was $24,045. OLDX is worth $29,515.05 today, giving her an actual profit of almost $6,000, and in the next year, she could have expected another $1,400 in income. This amazing and effective illusion makes a pretty solid investment look terrible. She has a profit of almost $6,000, but the Money Magicians keep showing her a loss of $6,000. The bottom line is that if you reinvest dividends, which can often be a very smart investment move, you will no longer get to see what you originally paid to buy the position listed meaningfully on your statement. Instead, the Money Magicians set up our statements so that our dividend profit masquerades as principal in a very powerful illusion that affects almost every investor.

How does the statement hide your rebalancing profit?

Any time profit has been used to automatically buy more investments, there are two very different glasses on the table, because one is principal and one is profit. But the audience is encouraged to see them as exactly the same so that Wall Street can keep up with IRS tax reporting. This scenario doesn't just occur when reinvesting dividends. It also occurs whenever Wall Street rebalances a portfolio.

To "rebalance" means to bring the percentage of each investment in a portfolio back to where it started. For example, let's use five stocks that are each 20 percent of a portfolio at the start of the year. It doesn't matter how much money they are worth as long as they each are 20 percent of the total. Over time, they can go up and down, making them bigger or smaller, which means they each are no longer exactly 20 percent of the total. At that time, Wall Street can rebalance the portfolio, which means it sells the higher ones that passed 20 percent and uses that money to buy the lower ones, which fell below 20 percent. After rebalancing, all positions are back to the original allocation, meaning each investment is worth 20 percent of the total again. Usually, technology lets investors rebalance automatically, and it happens based on either a calendar schedule or the amount of disparity among the holdings. Rebalancing is often described as an automated way to buy low and sell high, and it can be a very powerful tool in managing one's finances.

But as Sally's situation has shown us, it can create problems with how the Money Magicians report the results to us. Looking back at Table 4.2, Sally and Tony both thought that she had doubled her investment in BBB and had lost almost $3,000 in AAA. But that's not correct at all, and yet how can we know that? The truth of Sally's profit would be a lot more obvious if she could easily see the money the way she (and the rest of us) wants to see it. Where's her principal, the original investment she made with her hard-won savings? The Money Magicians ensure it takes some extra energy to identify and keep track of the original purchase. Once we know what Sally paid for each position originally, we can immediately see that she's made money in BBB and used that profit to buy more AAA, which is also profitable. That initial purchase is what matters, but all the major Wall Street firms make us search around a bit for that data.

In Table 4.7, I show how those 10 years could look if we saw Sally's data through a commonsense lens. She used $18,000 to buy both of those positions at $9,000 each. Now that you know what Sally actually paid for them (instead of what the IRS wants to consider taxable), the whole situation looks different. She has profit in both positions, and overall, her original $18,000 has turned into almost $25,000. She sold AAA because she thought it had lost almost $3,000 when, in reality, it had *gained over $3,000.*

Table 4.7 Rebalancing AAA and BBB

Year	AAA	BBB	Description	Shares AAA	AAA Value	Shares BBB	BBB Value	Total
2000	$30.00	$10.00	Initial purchase	300	$9,000.00	900	$9,000.00	$18,000.00
2001	$30.00	$11.00	Before rebalance	300	$9,000.00	900	$9,900.00	$18,900.00
			Selling $450 of BBB to buy AAA	315	$9450.00	860	$9,460.00	$18,910.00
2002	$30.00	$12.00	Before rebalance	315	$9,450.00	860	$10,320.00	$19,770.00
			Selling BBB to buy AAA	329	$9,870.00	824	$9,888.00	$19,758.00
2003	$30.00	$13.00	Before rebalance	329	$9,870.00	824	$10,712.00	$20,582.00
			Selling BBB to buy AAA	343	$10,290.00	792	$10,296.00	$20,586.00
2004	$30.00	$14.00	Before rebalance	343	$10,290.00	792	$11,088.00	$21,378.00
			Selling BBB to buy AAA	356	$10,680.00	764	$10,696.00	$21,376.00
2005	$30.00	$15.00	Before rebalance	356	$10,680.00	764	$11,460.00	$22,140.00
			Selling BBB to buy AAA	369	$11,070.00	739	$11,085.00	$22,155.00
2006	$30.00	$16.00	Before rebalance	369	$11,070.00	739	$11,824.00	$22,894.00
			Selling BBB to buy AAA	381	$11,430.00	716	$11,456.00	$22,886.00
2007	$30.00	$17.00	Before rebalance	381	$11,430.00	716	$12,172.00	$23,602.00
			Selling BBB to buy AAA	393	$11,790.00	695	$11,815.00	$23,605.00
2008	$30.00	$18.00	Before rebalance	393	$11,790.00	695	$12,510.00	$24,3000
			Selling BBB to buy AAA	405	$12,150.00	676	$12,168.00	$24,318.00
2009	$30.00	$19.00	Before rebalance	405	$12,150.00	676	$12,844.00	$24,994.00
			Selling BBB to buy AAA	416	$12,480.00	658	$12,502.00	$24,982.00
2010	$28.00	$20.00	Before rebalance	416	$12,480.00	658	$13,160.00	$24,808.0
			Selling BBB to buy AAA	443	$12,404.00	621	$12,420.00	$24,824.00

WHAT TO DO: AVOID THE SYSTEM, AVOID THE PROBLEMS

In Chapter 2, we discussed the fact that there is a basic, real-world difference between our purchase money and our dividend income. The first one is our principal, which we earn with our time and physical effort at a job. The second is our profit, which we earn from our investments, whether we got out of bed or not. None of the formats for any of Wall Street's statements reflect this important distinction.

Treating principal and profit the same in our monthly statements is a critically important part of tricking investors into doing more transactions. It's the deception that creates two different glasses on the magician's table. In one glass, people put their blood, sweat, and tears into saving their hard-earned money, and as is appropriate, they focus on not losing their principal. There's real money in that glass. However, in the other glass, the IRS uses a wrapper to trick us into thinking that it's full of the same kind of money because it wants to ensure that every cent, no matter how it's earned, gets captured as taxable.

People think, "I have a loss on that investment? I'm losing my hard-earned money here! That doesn't sound like a good investment, so I need to sell." This profit-over-principal approach to reporting is how people end up thinking an investment lost a lot of money when, in fact, the opposite is the case. Wall Street's statements fail to separate the purchases made with hard-earned principal versus purchases made with investment profit, and that forces people to look at their money from a tax-centric point of view. This is a serious problem because the investing public cannot clearly see how their investments are performing.

Over time, investors see this horribly inaccurate data and get fooled about the value of their investments just like the audience was tricked into believing the empty drinking glass was half full of money. Sally sold OLDX because it appeared to have lost $6,000 when it hadn't. The monthly statement hid the profit by suggesting that she's paid a lot more for OLDX than she really did. The audience thinks both glasses on the table are identical in the same way investors get fooled into thinking their principal is identical to their reinvested dividend profits.

ACTION STEP: Require your financial advisor to provide performance reporting that separates your principal from your profit.

By broadening the principal-oriented view from the position level to the account level, you can see how much principal is in that account as a whole, instead of each specific investment. The idea would be to clearly answer, "How much of my hard-earned savings have I put into this account?" The technology to provide this view of your portfolio already exists, and almost every financial firm has the capability to share it with you right now.

Therefore, investors should demand a principal-focused performance report at least once per year from their investment company. Properly done, that report clearly shows the money coming into and going out of the account ever since it was first opened (or at least going back many years). The idea is to make the profit earned obviously different from the principal deposited. Table 4.8 (which you first saw as Table 3.8 in Chapter 3) is a great example.

With a proper performance report like this, investors can clearly see their principal listed in the column titled "Additions." You can also make comparisons that help answer questions like, "Did I make more profit than I spent?" The answer to that question is found by simply comparing withdrawals with dividend income. In Table 4.8, we can see that the dividends created are more each year than the annual withdrawal. That's similar to saying, "I'm spending less than I am earning," which is an important goal for every household.

This report is currently very easy for Wall Street to provide, and the best financial advisors already offer it to their clients whenever discussing performance. If your advisor balks at providing this data,

Table 4.8 An Example of a Proper Performance Report

Time Period: 1/1/2014 to 12/31/2020

	Total Beginning Value	Additions	Withdrawls	Interest Income	Dividend Income	Period Realized Gains/Losses	Period Unrealized Gains/Losses	Total Ending Value	Return Percentage
1/1/2014 to 12/31/2014	$0.00	$2,939,068.61	$72,000.00	$19,808.78	$77,242.74	$13,118.27	$26,840.28	$3,004,078.68	4.56
1/1/2015 to 12/31/2015	$3,004,078.68	$0.00	$72,000.00	$17,206.54	$73,802.38	$22,180.76	$(181,034.85)	$2,864,233.51	-2.37
1/1/2016 to 12/31/2016	$2,864,233.51	$0.00	$72,000.00	$13,614.33	$83,012.96	$2,456.99	$181,968.55	$3,073,286.34	9.15
1/1/2017 to 12/31/2017	$3,073,286.34	$100,000.00	$72,000.00	$11,588.65	$92,810.56	$53,270.58	$82,392.96	$3,341,349.09	7.18
1/1/2018 to 12/31/2018	$3,341,249.09	$0.00	$72,000.00	$9,501.48	$95,321.10	$12,116.54	$(256,364.01)	$3,129,924.20	-4.45
1/1/2019 to 12/31/2019	$3,129,924.20	$0.00	$72,000.00	$9,627.61	$89,218.92	$40,176.49	$255,624.24	$3,452,571.46	11.43
1/1/2020 to 12/31/2020	$3,452,571.46	$50,000.00	$72,000.00	$7,756.01	$85,818.04	$22,707.69	$(96,052.72)	$3,450,800.48	0.59
Totals		$3,089,068.61	$504,000.00	$89,103.70	$597,226.40	$166,027.32	$13,374.45		

you might seriously consider looking for a new firm to handle your finances (but first read Part Two of this book, where I describe what to look for and what to avoid when working with Wall Street). By examining a proper performance report at least once per year, an investor can see the difference between principal and profit without the deceptive wrapper created by the Money Magicians.

ACTION STEP: Require your financial advisor to provide the percentage of income you receive based on your original investment.

If investors could easily see how much income they are earning in a way that aligns with their *principal making money* instead of *identifying gains/losses for taxes*, then people would do a lot of things differently. For example, let's say you bought a stock for $1,000 and every year it paid you $100 in income. That would be a nice 10 percent stream of dividend income that most people would not want to lose. But let's add a little more information to this scenario.

It's been 10 years since you bought that stock for $1,000. The first year, you reinvested the $100 income, which means you bought more of the stock and consequently had a bit more income the next year. That happened each year, and now with 10 years gone by, you have almost $2,400 invested in the stock. It's important to remember you only had to pay $1,000 out of your pocket originally for this, even though you won't be able to see that in the statement.

So far, this situation is very common because we bought a stock, held it for a few years, and reinvested the dividends. Let's add in one last bit of information to the scenario. Because 10 percent is such a good yield, the stock has gone up in value during the 10 years you've held it. People want to own a company that is so successfully paying its shareholders, and today, it's worth double what it was when you first bought it. How will you see that investment when you look at the statement Wall Street produces for you?

The first thing you'd see is that you have an approximate $1,600 gain, and the position is now worth a little over $4,000. That means Wall Street is telling you that you have a gain of about 70 percent. Also in the statement you'd see that the percentage of income you're earning is about 5 percent per year. The Money Magicians could call up their clients to declare, "Since it's only up 70 percent over 10 years, that's just 7 percent per year. And your percentage yield has gone down. You used to make 10 percent a year! Are you sure you want to hold on to this?"

And that description would be accurate, strictly speaking, which is why it's extremely misleading. If you use common sense instead of a tax-centric point of view, you only paid $1,000 for something that is worth over $4,000. That's a profit of over 400 percent! What's more, since you reinvested your dividends over that decade, you kept buying additional shares of the stock. With a greater amount of stock (that didn't cost you any hard-earned principal by the way), you are receiving more income. That first year you made $100 in income. The second year you made about $110 in income, and the income you earned kept getting higher and higher each year as you reinvested the dividends.

Today, you make over $230 in income, and Wall Street shows you this data in the worst possible light. Because the position is worth over $4,000, Wall Street says that the $230 you receive is about a 5 percent yield. That's accurate mathematically, but it's horribly deceptive. Remember, all you put in was $1,000 at the start. An income of $230 a year on an original investment of $1,000 is 23 percent! While Wall Street tries to convince you that you're getting a 5 percent yield, those of us who use common sense will agree that a 23 percent yield on the original investment looks pretty good.

The Money Magicians say you've got a 70 percent gain and a 5 percent yield, but when we pull back the curtain, it's a 400 percent gain and a 23 percent yield. This is why you must ask your advisory team to show you the yield on your original investment. A reasonable way to approach this is to ask for the statistics in writing during your annual review with your advisor. Every investment advisor today has the tools to be able to show clients the overall portfolio yield based on what you deposited into each account. That's going to be a much different number than you're used to seeing, which will spark new conversations and improved strategy discussions.

ACTION STEP: Keep your own records of how much you paid for your investments.

Because the original investment is so important, it is critical to keep track of it. If you don't work with a financial advisor, an obvious way to do that is to keep a spreadsheet of your own records. I know this isn't a fun solution, and most people will not enjoy doing it, but it's an effective work-around for those who have the time, the desire, and a comfort with numbers. For each investment, you could record the date you bought it and the amount you invested. Then, you'd want to keep track, on at least an annual basis, of the amount of income the position paid to you and what percentage yield that is based on your original investment. The downside to this approach is that it can become a very unwieldy, time-consuming project, which is why it might make a lot more sense to have your brokerage or investment advisor do it for you.

ACTION STEP: Meaningfully communicate that investment statement reporting standards must change.

It's going to require serious, industrywide change to solve the problem of seeing your money without the Money Magicians warping your view. The issue, as it stands now, is that Wall Street's statements and online views completely fail to characterize purchases in a way that customers want to see them. We need an investment statement that supports this basic truth: Something you buy with profit is different from something you buy with your principal.

If you explain to your banker or investment advisor that you want him to send a formal complaint up his chain of command, he will listen. The more people who demand a statement that prioritizes investors and their need to see the principal that they've invested, the more that someone on Wall Street might listen. A change like this will require major improvement across the entire industry's reporting infrastructure, and that's not likely to happen without your serious commitment to communicating the importance of this.

If you use social media, regardless of the platform, I highly encourage you to take advantage of the voice you have there. Here are a few tweets or posts that you might consider putting out there:

> Wall St's investment statements show our taxable profit, and that's not the same as our #ActualProfit. I'm tired of the #MoneyMagicians tricking us!

> #ActualProfit is not the same as the taxable gain or loss numbers on our investment statements. The #MoneyMagicians need to do better!

> Whichever Wall St firm first shows us #ActualProfit will get an enormous lead on the competition because that's what we want to see.

> Instead of only serving the IRS, Wall St should track and report principal-focused data because we want to see #ActualProfit.

> Pics get faked, text is from AI, and Wall St doesn't give #ActualProfit! It gives us taxable profit. I stand for authenticity and transparency!

> It's time for the #MoneyMagicians to report to us so we can see our investments from a tax-centric view *and* a principal-focused view.

The Money Magicians have other tricks up their sleeves, and the next chapter will describe how tax brackets and tax deductions have become so misunderstood. People often say, "I don't want to be in a higher tax bracket. I'm paying so much to the government; I need some deductions to lower my taxes!" But the trick is on them, because those statements only make sense if you've been duped into ignoring the money in your pocket while you focus solely on what the IRS takes from you. If you were clearly tracking the money you get to keep (the funds you can hold on to or use however you wish), you probably would never say those things. Chapter 5 explores why.

DISILLUSION

HERE'S HOW THE RETIREE GETS TRICKED INTO SELLING GOOD INVESTMENTS

Retirees want steady income. They need their portfolios to create income so they can pay the bills and enjoy vacations. That means that many of their investments pay them interest and dividends that they can use to meet their lifestyle needs. When they look at how much a stock pays them each year in dividends, the only data field on the statement that might help is entitled "Yield." Unfortunately, the Money Magicians have doctored this field so that it doesn't show what people think it shows.

For example, if you spend $100 to buy a stock and it pays you $5 a year, then you are getting a 5 percent yield. But as time passes and the value of that stock goes up and down, the yield listed on your statement changes as well. Nothing else has changed. You still only paid $100 to buy the position, and you are still getting $5 each year. But the Money Magicians show you the yield based on the *price you get if you sell the stock.* This is a transaction-focused perspective instead of a principal-focused one.

It can be even more misleading if the retiree bought the stock for $100 twenty years ago and reinvested dividends all that time before she recently retired. With all those reinvested dividends, which didn't cost her anything by the way, she has double the number of shares she started with, and so she's making double the income. It used to be, she made $5 a year, but now she makes about $10 a year; and in comparison with her original investment of $100, that's a wonderful yield of 10 percent. But she will never see 10 percent listed on her statement, because an accurate description of her income will not encourage her to sell.

To trick her into doing more transactions, the Money Magicians show her a yield that's less than half of that true, principal-focused yield. The bottom line here is that the Money Magicians show you the yield calculated using the value of the position at that moment in time. This means that as the position goes up in value, you see a smaller and smaller yield reported on the statement even though you're still getting the same amount of income from your original investment (which remains unchanged). In this way, yield is just another plastic costume around our portfolio, deceiving us into seeing something that isn't there.

5

THE MIND-CONTROL ILLUSION

Have You Been Hypnotized by the IRS?

"For this next trick, I'll need some volunteers," the magician announces with a flourish of his cape. "Are there any children in the audience who like quarters? Because if you can use quarters in your life, you are going to want to raise your hand." You look around the auditorium at all the little kids straining with their hands in the air as high as they can raise them. A few of them are standing and jumping up and down trying to get the magician to pick them.

"If you have your hand up, then come to the stage, and we'll get situated for my next trick." You sense a happy feeling of surprise ripple through the audience as every child who wants to participate starts to move toward the front. Assistants come from behind the curtain and position a row of tables across the stage. They set two chairs at opposite sides of each table so the occupants must face each other. The kids randomly take a seat, and you quickly count 15 tables with a total of 30 children. Meanwhile, the magician and his staff dump a pile of quarters in the middle of each table.

As the children get their own quiet instructions, the magician tells the audience, "I will now demonstrate my hypnotic and telepathic abilities by controlling the minds of these kids. You will see that I know what they intend to do without them saying a word to me. Each table has two random children sitting across from each other, and in between them is a pile of exactly 100 quarters. Which of the children will leave the money on the table and return to their seats with nothing? Which ones will take the money? I will divine the answer through powerful mind control as I orchestrate the entire thing from inside a sealed box."

THE ONSTAGE PERFORMANCE—WHY DON'T THEY KEEP THE MONEY?

The audience starts murmuring, and from your seat you can see the kids have received their instructions and are ready to begin. But you're wondering how this could be considered a trick at all. You think, "Every child went up there to get some money. Why would a child leave any quarters for the magician? Maybe some of the children were told they couldn't have the money?" After the magician closes himself in a box so he can't see anything, the kids on the left of each table make a split in the pile of coins. After making the split, the child on the right looks at what is being offered. Table after table, the kid on the left offers the kid on the right some amount of money. At one table, the offer is only a single quarter, and at another table, the money is split 50-50. The second child on the right of each table examines whatever split was made and marks something on a piece of paper, which is then folded so no one can read it.

Once this process is complete, the magician leaves his box, walks across the stage, and examines the two piles of quarters on each table while stroking his chin dramatically. The kids appear anxious. The audience seems to be holding its breath. Just when the tension feels unbearable, the magician takes action. He approaches the first table and announces, "They are taking the quarters!" The child on the right unfolds the paper, and the audience can see a big "YES" written there. The magician moves to the next table, where in a low and menacing voice, he says, "They won't be taking any of my money!"

The two kids at this table seem grumpy as the crowd sees the little sign displaying a clear "NO." The magician asks them, "You were allowed to take the quarters, yes?"

"Yes, sir," they reply.

"You chose of your own free will to leave the money for me. Is that right?"

"That's right."

The audience watches this happen again and again until, after 15 tables of accepted and rejected money, the magician bows, proving his mind-control powers are beyond reproach. *But how did he do it?* And more importantly, why didn't every child simply say, "Thank you," and go back to his or her seat with some money?

THE ALL-POWERFUL VIP PASS— WHAT YOU GET VERSUS WHAT I KEEP ON STAGE

You stand to signal that the show must stop, and you approach the stage where one of the assistants explains the situation to you. The secret to the trick lies in the instructions that were given to the kids. They were told to play a game with very specific roles and rules known as the "Ultimatum Game." It turns out, when people play this game, two things almost always occur: First, they become very predictable; and second, one of the players easily gets distracted from what is actually good for him or her. That player is usually the second person, who is the recipient of the "deal" being made by the first person. The second person predictably loses sight of what he or she truly wants, which in this case was the money. This wasn't mind control at all; it was a game—with a set of rules—that makes people do things they don't really want to do.

The Ultimatum Game was created in the early 1980s by a German named Werner Guth as an experiment in fairness and greed. Since then, many variations of the experiment have been completed, and for the most part, it's clear that as a result of the game, most people on one side of the table lose sight of their real goal. Here's how it works.

Two people at a table see a stack of something they each want. This is usually money, but it could be anything that both people want. Each person has a certain role to play in dividing the money (or food or whatever) between the two of them. The first person has the authority to make an offer to the second. That authority gives the first person a special power to make a split and decide how much money to keep and how much to offer to the second person. With this authority, the first person can pick any amount to offer the second, but once he makes his offer, his role in the game is complete.

The second person has a different role. She controls the right to approve or deny the split. If she approves, then they take their money and go. If she decides to deny the split, then no one gets anything. Overall, the first person in the Ultimatum Game tries to offer a division of value that the second person will accept, or no one will receive any of it.

Economists often suggest that people can be relied upon to act rationally. This means a random person, like one of the little girls on stage, should gravitate toward decisions that bring the most individual gain to herself. In that light, the second child who approves the split in the Ultimate Game should—logically speaking—accept any amount of money because it's a benefit to the child. Even if the second child only walks away with a single quarter, it's still more than the youngster had a moment ago.

But the Ultimatum Game experiments have shown that people do not behave this way in real life. Over and over again, the vast majority of players will deny a small offering and take nothing because they lose sight of their personal goal, which was to make more money. Instead, they focus on the unfairness of the overly large share that the other person gets to keep. Seeing an unfair split, the second person decides that no one will get anything.

OUTSIDE THE THEATER

Imagine two friends named Paul and Johnny. Let's assume Paul just found $100 in the street, but Johnny did not know that. Paul, feeling charitable, approaches his friend Johnny and says, "Hey friend, can I offer you a dollar, no strings attached?" Johnny would take that dollar every single time.

But if Paul and Johnny were playing the Ultimatum Game, a problem arises, because Johnny finds himself with power over Paul. He gets to approve or deny what Paul keeps for himself. In that case, Johnny gets distracted by his authority over Paul, and focuses on the fact that Paul is keeping $99. Johnny loses sight of the fact that accepting the offer of $1 is logically beneficial to him. It's a real-life example of one of the meanings behind the saying, "Power corrupts."

Even though Johnny could effortlessly make one extra dollar, he will likely deny a 99-to-1 split and lose the dollar to ensure Paul doesn't get to keep too much. Scientists say that this is hardwired into our nature as part of humankind's "social contract" and that the reason Johnny denies the offer is to teach Paul to split more fairly next time. Another way to look at it is that the Ultimatum Game tricks Johnny. As he loses sight of what logically benefits him, he stops thinking about his personal desire to collect some money, because the system gave him a kind of power over Paul. With that distraction, Johnny chooses to stop Paul from taking "too much" of the money while, at the same time, failing to improve his own situation.

When the split is 99 for Paul and 1 for Johnny, then the Johnnies of the world most likely vote down the lopsided split, and no one gets anything. The Ultimatum Game shows that when people feel the situation is unfair, they are inclined to punish the bad actor even if that causes loss for them as well. That's how the magician knew if the kids were going to keep any of the quarters. All he had to do was look at the number of coins each kid was offered. If the split was grossly unfair, human nature demanded that no one get anything.

The exact same thing happens every year as people pay their taxes. The IRS has set up its own (very complicated) version of the Ultimatum Game. People keep making financial decisions that leave them with less money because they're focused so intently on not letting the IRS take "too much" of their hard-won earnings. The IRS uses its formidable influence to take advantage of our natural tendencies so that we leave the table with less money, just like some of the kids on the stage.

THE REAL-LIFE PERFORMANCE—WHY DON'T THEY KEEP THE MONEY?

Edgar and Marianne are in their late forties and have two kids in college. Marianne is a saleswoman who works on commission, and Edgar works in banking. Together, their income is about $300,000 per year. But as is the case for all of us, taxes bite into that, and they don't get to take home $300,000. One day, Edgar is talking to his CPA, and he learns that he and his wife have been in the 24 percent tax bracket for years now. He knows there are higher brackets with more tax, but 24 percent feels like a lot to him.

"I wish we weren't in such a high tax bracket," Edgar laments. He calculates that 24 percent of $300,000 is over $70,000. "I am paying too much in taxes! There must be some way to lower that, because I know smart people aren't losing so much of their money to Uncle Sam. I need some deductions since that's the way people lower their taxes!"

Seeing her husband's frustration, Marianne says, "Well, I know one thing we can do. I can delay a big sale at work since I've maxed out my IRA and can't contribute any more savings there. By delaying the sale, that's $10,000 in commissions that won't come in until next year, so that should lower our taxable income this year."

"That's a great idea," says Edgar. "I forgot about those contribution limits on our retirement accounts. If we've hit those limits, that means we can't save any more money in there, so we need to do something else. Delaying your commission will definitely make our tax bill less."

Later that week, Edgar sees his neighbor Gary working in the garage and stops in to talk a bit. Gary is a CPA and a business owner, and Edgar is curious about his take on all this. When Edgar brings up the tax question, Gary says to him, "I remember you mentioned your wife wanted to start a home-based fitness business on the side, right? You should get that going, and then all the equipment or other costs associated with the business would be deductions and could help lower how much you pay in taxes."

Edgar tells Marianne about Gary's advice, and while she's not really enthusiastic about adding more to her plate, she's willing to do it if it will help them save money on taxes. That very night, they look online for some in-home exercise equipment that Marianne could use to coach some clients. They find what they need, and it costs about $10,000. For another $3,000, they get one of their cars wrapped with fancy advertising so that people might call Marianne and sign up for help with fitness and exercise. Finally, they spend another $2,000 on different kinds of marketing including a website and social media ads.

Even though Marianne never actually signs a client, they both are pleased to have taken action with purchases that can be deducted from their income, thereby lowering the taxable amount of money they made, which in turn lowers their tax bill. They congratulate each other because the $15,000 they spent, along with Marianne deferring a deal at work worth about $10,000 in commission, accomplished their goal, and they had some fun doing it. The next time Edgar is on the golf course with his friends, he mentions that he expects to save almost $15,000 on his taxes this year because Marianne's home business is giving them a lot of deductions. His friends all go home that day wondering if they should be doing the same thing.

But they should *not* do the same thing. No one should do this. Edgar and Marianne made some serious miscalculations because they lost sight of their real goal, which is to make more money. They didn't know it, but they played the Ultimatum Game with the IRS, which triggered their natural human tendency to exercise power over how much money the IRS can take. Let's examine how this happens so often and why it is harmful to your financial well-being.

THE ALL-POWERFUL VIP PASS— WHAT YOU GET VERSUS WHAT I KEEP IN REAL LIFE

"I don't want to be in a higher tax bracket. I'm paying so much to the government; I need some deductions to lower my taxes." It's the ultimate misconception! For this illusion to work, the IRS needs Edgar and Marianne to think about their income a lot like players do in the Ultimatum Game where most people will refuse a single dollar if the other person gets ninety-nine. People reject that dollar offer because they confuse two different goals: making money for themselves and keeping the other person from making money. But outside the Ultimatum Game, those same people would accept the dollar gift without a problem because it's logical and rational to make beneficial decisions. Everyone knows a gift of a single dollar is better than zero dollars, which means it's *the power to control what the other party gets* that creates confusion.

Tax brackets are a complex kind of Ultimatum Game because people have the power to work the system and try to be in certain tax brackets. Sadly, this usually is just a distraction from their real goal, which is simply to keep as much money as possible. As soon as Edgar saw he was in the 24 percent tax bracket, he was hooked into the trick. We know that because Edgar exclaims, "I wish we weren't in such a high tax bracket." With that one statement, he's missing two very important facts. *Fact number one: Making more money and being in a higher tax bracket does not change the tax you owe in the lower brackets.* The government charges the same tax within each bracket no matter how much you earn (we'll explore this more in a moment). *Fact number two: The higher your tax bracket, the more money you keep.* If you are in the highest tax bracket, you should celebrate, because you are likely making, and keeping, a lot more money than you otherwise would.

Edgar, like a lot of people, thought that making more money and getting into a higher tax bracket affected his finances badly. But the truth is that it doesn't hurt his finances at all unless he's upset that he made, and gets to keep, more money. This is because each tax bracket only affects those specific dollars being earned in that bracket. What that means is, if someone is in the 24 percent tax bracket and someone else is in the 32 percent tax bracket, their tax on the first part of their earnings is exactly the same. It can feel complicated, but if we look at the situation just a bit more, you'll see it's actually very straightforward.

We All Have the Same Tax on the First Part of Our Earnings

Brackets enclose something, and in this case, it's earned income. So a 10 percent bracket could enclose the income from $0 earned to $19,900 earned. That bracket is separate from the others like the levels of a fountain. Each basin of water, or in this case money, is separate from the rest. The next level on the fountain is the 12 percent bracket, which encloses the income from $19,901 to $81,050. Overall, it's a gradient system, where each level of the fountain is separate from the others.

In this gradient system, your fountain fills up the first level to $19,900; then it starts to fill up the next level until you reach $81,050. The 12 percent rate of tax only applies to the dollars in that second level of the fountain. The 12 percent rate does not apply to the earned income below $19,901 because that money is taxed at 10 percent. Nor does the 12 percent rate apply to money above $81,050 because those dollars are spilling into the next level of the fountain, which will have a higher rate.

In Table 5.1, "Simple Tax Brackets," we see three people and their tax situations. Person A made $19,900, which puts her in the lowest tax bracket of 10 percent. This means that after she pays the tax, she keeps $17,910, which is exactly the same amount of money the next two people keep *within that tax bracket*. Person B makes $20,000, which puts her in the 12 percent tax bracket. Edgar would think that jumping up to the next bracket is a serious problem, but we can see that it's not. Person B keeps more money after taxes than Person A because the tax of 12 percent is only applied to the dollars *within that tax bracket*. Person C makes the most money and is squarely in the 12 percent tax bracket, but her tax on the first $19,900 is exactly the same as that of the other two people.

Table 5.1   Simple Tax Brackets

Person A earns $19,900 this year				
Tax Bracket	Tax Rate	Dollars Earned	Tax Collected	Earnings Kept
$0–$19,900	10%	$19,900	$1,990	$17,910
$19,901–$81,050	12%	$0	$0	$0
Total	10%	$19,900	$1,990	$17,910
Person B earns $20,000 this year				
Tax Bracket	Tax Rate	Dollars Earned	Tax Collected	Earnings Kept
$0–$19,900	10%	$19,900	$1,990	$17,910
$19,901–$81,050	12%	$100	$12	$88
Total	10.01%	$20,000	$2,002	$17,998
Person C earns $30,000 this year				
Tax Bracket	Tax Rate	Dollars Earned	Tax Collected	Earnings Kept
$0–$19,900	10%	$19,900	$1,990	$17,910
$19,901–$81,050	12%	$10,100	$1,212	$8,888
Total	10.67%	$30,000	$3,202	$26,798

Let's go over that again from another point of view. All three people paid the exact same tax on the first $19,900 that they made. The tax bill on the first $19,900 doesn't change whether they make a lot more money or not. The higher tax rates are only applicable to the dollars earned in each of those higher brackets. What this means is that earning enough money to be in a higher tax bracket is typically a good thing and should be a financial goal for most Americans.

Consider that the entire "tax bracket conversation" is set up to focus on what taxpayers lose and not on what they keep. So right at the start, the public's perspective is framed as, "Here's what I have to give up to the IRS." All the tax forms and reporting documents highlight what must be paid to the IRS, which means the public rarely is even aware of the more important information: the amount of money they can keep and use freely. That sounds a lot like the Ultimatum Game, where the second person judges what the first person gets instead of just looking at what can be gained. It's important to focus on what you are able to take home and freely spend however you wish.

Deductions Lower What You Keep by a Lot and Lower Your Taxes by a Little

There is an incredible amount of social pressure in America to avoid getting into a higher tax bracket because people confuse the goal of making more money with the goal of keeping the IRS from getting money. The Money Magicians use this pressure to entice people to try to seek out deductions. Sadly, people often misunderstand how deductions work and why their tax bill is less. The confusion stems from people focusing on their tax bill instead of the money they've earned, which is truly theirs to keep.

Person B in Table 5.1 made $20,000, which puts her in the 12 percent tax bracket. If she just pays her tax, then she keeps $17,998. But let's pretend she's upset like Edgar. She's accustomed to being in the 10 percent bracket, and now she's frustrated because she mistakenly thinks she must pay 12 percent tax on all her money. The table shows us that her total tax is only 10.01 percent. That's because she, like every other taxpayer, only pays 10 percent on the dollars in the 10 percent bracket. But with her mistaken focus on that 12 percent tax bracket, she thinks, "I need some deductions!"

In order to get those deductions, she pulls out her checkbook and spends her money—let's say $1,000—on something she wouldn't have normally bought. She doesn't need to buy this stuff, and she's spending that $1,000 specifically to stop the IRS from getting "too much." Let's say she does her homework, and her purchase legitimately creates a deduction that really does lower her taxable income, which, in turn, lowers her taxes. She might tell a friend that she lowered her taxes by about $1,000 the way Edgar said he lowered his taxes by $15,000 at the golf course. Sadly, Person B and Edgar are both wrong because they are too focused on the tax paid instead of how much they get to keep.

The math for deductions is simple as long as you keep your eye on what stays in your pocket (which people typically don't do). According to Table 5.1, Person B earned $20,000 overall. If she did nothing and simply earned her $20,000 and paid her taxes, then she'll pay $2,002 in taxes. This means she gets to keep $17,998. That's an important number because it's what she keeps if she doesn't mess around with trying to get deductions.

Now, let's start over with the same $20,000 overall, except this time, Person B spends $1,000 on something that gets a deduction, or "write-off" as it's sometimes called. The IRS's Ultimatum Game works wonders as she tells her friends, "I'm so happy, because after spending $1,000 on a legitimate write-off, only $19,000 of my earned income is taxable. And guess what? I lowered my tax bracket! Now, I only pay 10 percent." If someone tells her she's been tricked, she'd exclaim, "I haven't been tricked! I'm in the 10 percent tax bracket now, and 10 percent of $19,000 is $1,900, which means I'm sending less money to the IRS! I used to have to send over $2,000 to the IRS. With that $1,000 deduction, I lowered my taxes from $2,002 to $1,900. The IRS won't get as much." And she's absolutely right!

But was that really her goal? Maybe she just walked away from a table covered in quarters after rejecting the split of money. To clearly see that, we have to look at how much she gets to keep and spend however she wishes. *Spoiler alert:* She's left with less! She started with $20,000 total earnings, spent $1,000 buying deductions she normally wouldn't buy, and had to pay $1,900 in taxes, which leaves $17,100.

This is the trick. Before she let the IRS deceive her into spending money on stuff she otherwise wouldn't have, she had $17,998. Unfortunately, she was duped into buying things she didn't really need, and the result is that she only has $17,100.

The Money Magicians are tricking us into being consumers when we otherwise could save and grow our net worth. Instead of saving their money, Americans are being deceived into spending their extra savings. What's more, the purchases we make when we seek deductions like this are especially manipulative because the government that's taxing us is the same government that creates the list of the purchases that qualify for a deduction.

Don't Lower Your Taxes a Little by Giving Up a Lot of What You Could Keep

Let's reexamine what really happened for Edgar and Marianne, and this time we'll focus on what they get to keep. Remember, they started out making $300,000 a year. If we can take our focus off what the IRS gets and instead look at what Edgar and Marianne keep, we can see in Table 5.2 that by simply doing nothing, they have $239,958 to use however they wish. They could buy things that make them happy, or they could save however they feel best increases their net worth. That's almost $240,000, which they control and can freely use in whatever way pleases them.

Unfortunately, Edgar got tricked into thinking he pays 24 percent of every dollar in taxes because he was told he's in the 24 percent tax bracket. But we know he doesn't pay 24 percent tax on every dollar. That level of tax only applies to the dollars within that specific tax bracket. This means his overall tax is not greater than $70,000 as he exclaimed. The actual tax is a lot less. Table 5.2 shows it's only about 20 percent of his total earnings.

Table 5.2   Edgar and Marianne Before Deductions

Tax Bracket	Tax Rate	Dollars Earned	Tax Collected	Earnings Kept
$0–$19,900	10%	$19,900	$1,990	$17,910
$19,901–$81,050	12%	$61,150	$7,338	$53,812
$81,051–$172,750	22%	$91,700	$20,174	$71,526
$172,751–$329,850	24%	$127,250	$30,540	$96,710
Total	20.01%	$300,000	$60,042	$239,958

To summarize, Edgar and Marianne keep about $240,000. They pay about $60,000 in taxes, which is $10,000 less than they thought. And their effective tax rate is only about 20 percent. Unfortunately, Edgar got frustrated about how much he thought the IRS was getting in the split, and he decided to exert some power and authority over what the IRS gets. That's what deductions are: the illusion of power over how much the other person gets, which—as we know from the Ultimatum Game—distracts people from their own benefit.

What did Edgar and his wife do with their power? To start off, Marianne delayed closing a sale, so she didn't make $10,000 in commissions. Additionally, they spent about $15,000 on a home business. Marianne wasn't excited about doing the work for the exercise business, but she was willing to do it as a team player if it helped lower their taxes.

Said another way, they decided to ignore their own benefit and make it their mission to "punish" the IRS. The IRS Ultimatum Game plugs the public into trying to stop the government from getting money, and Marianne's first step was to put off some work so she didn't earn $10,000 that she otherwise could have. The second step Edgar made was to buy about $15,000 in business-related expenses. Table 5.3 shows how much they made after deductions, and the figure at the bottom right of the table shows how badly they were tricked.

"I haven't been tricked," exclaims Edgar. "My wife did not collect her commission in this tax year, which lowered our taxable income.

Then we spent some of our extra money on a home business that gave us legitimate deductions. Because of that, we truly lowered our taxes by about $6,000. I did what I wanted to do and successfully kept money from the IRS." And he's absolutely correct!

Table 5.3   Edgar and Marianne After Deductions

Tax Bracket	Tax Rate	Dollars Earned	Tax Collected	Earnings Kept
$0–$19,900	10%	$19,900	$1,990	$17,910
$19,901–$81,050	12%	$61,150	$7,338	$53,812
$81,051–$172,750	22%	$91,700	$20,174	$71,526
$172,751–$329,850	24%	$102,250	$24,540	$77,710
Total	19.65%	$275,000	$54,042	$220,958

But is that really what they wanted? How much money did they get to keep and use however they please? They started with $300,000 total possible earnings, delayed making $10,000, and spent $15,000 buying deductions they normally wouldn't buy. After these actions, they had to pay $54,042 in taxes, leaving them with only $220,958 to use, save, and enjoy in whatever way they wished. That's about $20,000 less!

They were tricked, and in talking about it at the golf course with friends, Edgar was unknowingly deceiving his friends as well. Before Marianne and Edgar let the IRS deceive them into spending money on stuff they really didn't need, they had almost $20,000 in additional funds to use as they wished. Before they were duped into playing the IRS Ultimatum Game, that $20,000 was rightfully theirs. What if they had saved that money instead?

WHAT TO DO: AVOID THE SYSTEM, AVOID THE PROBLEMS

Edgar and Marianne sought deductions because they couldn't save any more money in their retirement plans. Currently, regulators use contribution limits to make sure that individuals cannot save too much of their money in retirement plans (and *that* seems to be a very clear statement about the real systemic goal being pushed on the public). The Money Magicians encourage individuals to play the Ultimatum Game because they need society to continue to spend and consume. With those limits on the amount they can save in retirement accounts, the government removes our ability to make tax-deferred savings of whatever amount we wish, which is a powerful motivator for consumerism.

It's easier for consumerism to flourish when people don't have a tax incentive to save beyond a contribution limit. This environment creates more transaction-minded citizens. Those contribution limits also take away people's ability to truly lower their tax bill. Enforcing a limit on how much people can save in retirement plans is a powerful way to make sure Americans stay plugged into the IRS's Ultimatum Game because we're not allowed to save "too much" of our money in retirement accounts that truly lower our taxes.

Unfortunately, Edgar and Marianne used up hours of their life focused on spending their money on transactions for exercise equipment and other things. The government can benefit from people being consumers like this because those transactions probably generated sales tax and income tax for the businesses that sold them those items. That means the government got more money while Edgar and Marianne gave up theirs. Instead of just saving their money, they played the Ultimatum Game with the IRS, and every year that they do this, they will be less wealthy and less financially secure.

ACTION STEP: Make your voice heard politically if you wish to influence how much the IRS collects.

After decades of working with individuals seeking to grow their net worth, I've come to believe the following: A lot of the maneuvering people do trying to lower their tax bill only happens because they feel driven to exercise power over the IRS or the government in general. Most people feel so helpless when actively participating in the nation's political process that it's refreshing to exercise a little control over their taxes (even if it hurts them financially).

If you feel the IRS should collect less taxes, there are other ways to address that without giving up your hard-earned money. Unfortunately, most people don't feel the political process hears their voice, and that makes them more susceptible to this particular illusion. Because it requires a lot of difficult work and patience to effectively impact the government, people are easily tricked into fast, ineffective solutions like spending money on IRS-approved deductions. The less that people are involved in their government and the political process, the more likely they are prone to try to exercise "power" at tax time by making poor decisions that hurt their financial standing.

To truly change the amount the IRS collects from the public requires some political involvement. A great way to get started is to take a glance at websites like USDebtClock.org, FiscalData.Treasury.gov, and USASpending.gov. After that, if you're interested in making meaningful change to America's budget, you might consider joining a group like the Concord Coalition, which was started by both Republicans and Democrats and offers many excellent ways to make an impact on this nation's financial discussion.

ACTION STEP: Tell your political leaders that our nation's debt and national deficit are not acceptable.

Supporting the Concord Coalition is a great first step, but toward what goal? If you wish to pay less money to the government, then you might try paying more attention to the reason the IRS collects taxes in the first place. Simply put, the American government collects taxes to provide a certain level of support to its citizens. People are going to disagree about which services are important, and they will argue about the amount of support the government should provide.

And that's OK! This debate is part of the foundation of a diverse American political spectrum that supports our successful democracy. But whether you are more liberally inclined or conservative in nature, we can all agree that excessive debt and disproportionate government spending is not in the interest of anyone who would like to keep more of their hard-won earnings in their pockets.

Right now, America spends more than it collects in taxes. This is the deficit, and each year that the United States spends money it doesn't have, it adds to our national debt. If you wish to influence how much the government takes in taxes, a great way to start is by communicating with your voted leaders in politics. You can identify them using the "Find your representatives" tool provided by the non-partisan group Common Cause. At www.commoncause.org, you'll find an organization dedicated to making sure people's voices are heard by their leaders. You can use the website to connect with your leaders on social media and to reach out to them via email and letters.

You and I both need to get more involved in the political process and demand that our local and national leadership stop spending more money than they bring in through taxes. When the amount the government spends each year is clearly below what the country collects in taxes, then the nation could start paying down the $31 trillion debt. As the national debt gets smaller, our country's financial status becomes more stable, and we, as a people, have a real chance to talk about collecting less taxes. Until then, the Money Magicians are sure to continue to use the Ultimatum Game as a necessary and effective tool to collect as much money as possible.

Said another way, Wall Street and the IRS are encouraging Americans to consume as much as possible because our nation is overspending and deeply in debt. The more you think you need deductions, the more you will go spend your money. And the way you are spending all that money is going to be in accordance with the rules the government created so you can be tricked into thinking that lowering your tax bill is the same as keeping more money.

ACTION STEP: Instead of trying to change the entire tax code, lower individual taxes by demanding the removal of contribution limits on tax-deferred saving.

If you're in communication with your voted representatives, what would you say to them? The deficit and national debt are such big problems that it seems like most of the solutions involve starting over with a renovation of the entire system. There are a couple of popular "overhaul" ideas that keep popping up in this debate. For those of us on the extreme liberal side of the political spectrum, the story is to endorse a value-added tax similar to that in European countries. For the most conservative among us, the approach is nearly the exact opposite and involves a flat tax that everyone must pay.

Why don't we hear anything about a more workable approach that doesn't require a complete overhaul? The reason is the IRS Ultimatum Game that keeps us focused on the brackets and the deductions. If the debate isn't about a complete overhaul, then everyone is arguing about how to change the Ultimatum Game instead of just refusing to play it. We've all heard questions like, "Should the numbers used in the tax brackets be a 10 percent tax on the first $19,000 or an 11 percent tax on the first $22,000?" Our current gradient system provides an endless debate over the millions of ways we could arrange the tax brackets and the percentages each bracket charges.

Similarly, there's an infinity of ways to restructure deductions. Should a business meal be deducted, and if so, what percentage of the meal? Should the interest on your home mortgage be deductible? What about the cost of the gas you use to drive to check on your rental house? This debate on how to structure the rules has been happening our entire lives, and it's an illusion of individual power because the overall Ultimatum Game remains intact.

There's a better way that no one ever talks about. It's an effective and easy way to slightly alter our tax code that would allow both sides of the political aisle to benefit. If implemented, this simple change would empower individuals to keep more money in their pockets each year, and it would lower their taxes that year as well. In fact, it gives genuine authority to people to determine how much tax they pay in direct connection to how much they save for their future. *I'm talking about the elimination of contribution limits in IRAs and 401(k) plans.*

When you put your money into a retirement plan, you are keeping your funds, not spending them on deductions. This is individually beneficial because the funds are still yours and—this should please people who don't want the IRS to get any money—those savings aren't taxed the year you earned them. But right now, the IRS limits how much money the public can put into those plans. If those limits were removed, people wouldn't have to mess around with deductions. Instead, they could lower their taxes by choosing to save for the future, which is almost always a smart choice at both the individual and national level.

Removing these limits empowers individuals to control their tax bill because each household could determine how much it wishes to save. The government would still get its tax dollars, albeit in the future, because the funds will get taxed when they come out of the retirement plan later in life. If people truly wanted to effectively lower their taxes with an easy, nonpolitical change, they'd get started immediately by asking their leaders to remove the contribution limits on retirement plans. If you are on social media, why not post this right now: "After reading *Outsmart the Money Magicians*, I support removing the contribution limits to IRAs and 401(k) plans because it empowers people to grow their net worth while lowering their taxes." If you'll tag me on Facebook, LinkedIn, and/or X (formerly Twitter), I'd love to support your post.

ACTION STEP: Each year, focus more on the amount of money you make and keep rather than on what you end up paying the IRS.

There is a difference between trying to increase your net worth and trying to keep the IRS from collecting too much money. The first one is accomplished, mathematically speaking, by focusing on earning as much as possible and, as a consequence, paying more taxes. By looking at increasing the money we earn and keep, it changes our experience in the same way that accepting the gift of $1 feels different from approving someone else getting to keep the other $99.

It's hard to accept, but a good rule of thumb is, "The bigger the tax bill, the more money you get to keep." This common misunderstanding about the American gradient tax bracket system makes it all the more vital to actively avoid playing the Ultimatum Game with the IRS. With that accomplished, you can take an important step in the direction of earning additional money and keeping more of it every year. By reading this book, you are already better informed because you understand the perils of getting hooked into trying to use spur-of-the-moment deductions to keep the IRS from collecting taxes.

When people get tricked into the Ultimatum Game, they often hurt themselves financially because they are trying to hurt the IRS. Mathematically speaking, it's an irrational goal to lower the money you get to keep in order to stop the IRS from getting funds. We all should remember, "The more you make, the more you keep. So try to make more money!" It makes a lot of sense to *focus your energies on activities that increase your income.* For now, it's enough to know that spending money you otherwise wouldn't and trying to make less money are both flawed approaches to bettering your financial picture because you likely will end up with a smaller amount of money.

Try to keep your attention on what stays in your pocket. Doing so will help you to unplug from the "be a consumer" machine, which is a problem for people trying to grow their net worth. The extra money that you will get to keep can be used to maximize your net worth now that this powerful illusion no longer tricks you.

DISILLUSION

HERE'S A LOOK AT THE TAX ADVISOR VERSUS
THE INVESTMENT ADVISOR

Have you ever heard someone brag about how great his tax return was prepared? It's much more common to hear people calling attention to their investment triumphs. The problem is that this is backward. People should pay much more attention to their taxes.

In the pecking order of importance, the tax advisor trumps the investment advisor every time. There are a number of reasons for this, but let's just focus on the three biggest ones. First, the tax advisor helps you keep what you've already earned. If you can lower your tax bill in a meaningful way (as opposed to the flawed approaches we just went over in this chapter), that's real money that never leaves your pocket.

The second reason your tax advisor is more important than your investment advisor boils down to percentages. If a tax advisor is able to significantly lower your taxes, that could be a savings of 20 to 40 cents off every dollar earned. An investment advisor is doing excellent work if she accomplishes a profit of 10 cents on every dollar. These ratios are always skewed in favor of the tax advisor.

Lastly, it's meaningful to consider which advisor's mistakes will most adversely affect you. For the investment advisor, the typical "worst-case scenario" is that the portfolio temporarily drops 20 to 50 percent. During that time, you are free to continue working and living your life, albeit with the stress of wondering when your portfolio will get back to the value it once was. Contrast that with the tax advisor, where if something goes wrong, it could result in your incarceration or the seizure of your assets. Jail trumps investment declines every time.

What this all means is that an excellent investment advisor should be in touch with your tax advisor. There's no wrong way for an investment expert to liaison with her client's tax expert, as long as there's some meaningful, repeatable interaction. Sometimes that's as simple as letting the client know that the tax documents from the portfolio have been given to the tax advisor. Or it could be an annual meeting between the two different advisors to go over the shared client's financial model. If your financial advisor isn't regularly in touch in a meaningful way with your tax advisor, then that's a request you could make that can dramatically increase the effectiveness of the members of your financial team as they work toward your future objectives.

PART TWO

THE THEATER, DECONSTRUCTED

WHAT'S INSIDE

A description of the system itself to include:

- The typical experience people have when working with a brokerage financial advisor

- The advisor-specific mechanisms that put customers at a disadvantage

- The broker-specific procedures that create conflicts of interest and poor customer service

- Detailed action steps for how to keep the upper hand when working with Wall Street

In Part One of this book, I pulled the curtain back on the top five illusions performed by the IRS and Wall Street. In Part Two, I take the spotlight off the stage magician and instead direct your attention to the theater itself. There are a lot of trap doors, hidden rooms, magnets, and mirrors that serve to distract and disorient the audience. Where Part One addressed basic systemic bias, Part Two dives into the actual conflicts of interest and different legal levels of service provided. Part One addressed how to understand and manage your money, but here in Part Two, we'll examine how Wall Street treats the customer—you.

The four chapters that follow focus on how Wall Street brokerages approach both their work and their customers. My goal is to empower the public so that you, the reader, can successfully demand that these investment houses do better. We'll discuss how and why brokerages regularly engage with their clients. At best, the relationship between Main Street and Wall Street is vaguely unsatisfactory, and at worst it's a grave and unjust misalignment that benefits the brokerages far more than the clients.

When it comes to major Wall Street brokerages, the main message is, "Avoid the system, avoid the problems." In Chapter 6, I'll introduce you to Rick and Rachel and share their story as they hire and fire financial advisors. Then, I'll take the theater apart piece by piece in the next two chapters so you can see the litany of systemic conflicts of interest that benefit Wall Street and do not help Main Street. Finally, I'll close Part Two by describing in detail how to engage with Wall Street and your financial advisor *to your advantage*.

6

THE TYPICAL EXPERIENCE

Working with a Wall Street Financial Advisor

I remember, years ago, a couple friends of mine hired a magician to entertain a group of six-year-olds at their daughter's birthday party. They asked neighbors for recommendations and looked them up online. After a basic internet search, they decided on Tommy the Magician. His website had great photos, some testimonials and comments, and an easy-to-use booking tool.

His website collected his fee up front, which automated a calendar to pop up so they could select the date and time Tommy the Magician would arrive. As it got closer to the party, they'd hoped to change the time, but there really was no way to do that; and when they called, they had to leave a message and never got a response. When he arrived at the originally booked time, Tommy looked more like a strange superhero clown than a magician, but he was otherwise very professional. My friends asked for two hours, and he arrived on time and left on time. But he didn't do a single magic trick. Instead, he made balloon animals, played music, and painted the little girls' faces.

It was an acceptable party because the kids enjoyed themselves and there were some great moments for pictures. My friends weren't dissatisfied exactly, but it wasn't what they'd really wanted. Certainly, it wasn't what they thought they were going to get. Talking with them about it, I thought they had relied on the fact that his business title was "magician," and then they filled in the blanks based on what they thought that title meant. If they had known there was no way to alter the time after booking, they might have done things a little differently, but it wasn't a disaster.

The relationship between clients and Wall Street's brokerages is similar to this interaction with Tommy the Magician in that it's not a complete disaster, but it is flawed in meaningful ways. Through the next several chapters, we'll follow Rachel and Rick and their family as we explore their experience working with different Wall Street financial advisors. Throughout the entire experience, which lasted many years, they did not know they were at such a disadvantage in the business relationship.

MEET RICK AND RACHEL: HIRING THEIR FINANCIAL ADVISOR

Married for many years and with two teenage kids, Rick is in his mid-thirties and has just gotten great news. He's earned a promotion in his job as a hospital administrator. His wife, Rachel, runs a successful home-based business helping people get more organized. The two of them have been mindful to keep their lifestyle inexpensive so they could save their money, and now with a higher income, Rachel suggests they hire a financial advisor who could help them manage their savings. Their first step is an internet search "financial advisors near me." Three nearby advisors pop up. But then Rachel remembers that her older sister's best friend, Donna, is a financial advisor, so that's who they call first.

Donna works at First Brokerage, and during their meeting, she explains that she will keep the couple informed of what's going on, and if something comes up, she will be proactive about reaching out to them. Rachel and Rick fill out a risk profile questionnaire in order to begin working with Donna, who, while taking their answers to 10 multiple-choice questions, mentions that the firm has a full-time CPA on staff who can do their taxes. Rick and Rachel are loyal to their current CPA, Francine, but they're thankful for the information.

Donna moves on to explain that Rick and Rachel will have access to some of the world's best money managers because of First Brokerage's special relationships on Wall Street. Donna believes there's a particular third-party, institutional investment team that would be an excellent fit for their family. Donna lays out her plan to split Rick and Rachel's money in half so that this special, top-notch Wall Street management team can supervise 50 percent of the funds while Donna directly oversees the other half. Rachel was impressed to learn that they normally couldn't work with institutional managers like these experts because these elite managers only handle really large, wealthy clients. Luckily, through First Brokerage, they get access to these exclusive Wall Street managers even though Rick and Rachel only have a fraction of what is typically required. What's more, First Brokerage has offices all over the country, and as everyone says, "The bigger, the better."

Despite their perfunctory internet search, Rick and Rachel decide that Donna's similar age and close ties to the family make her a good fit, so they don't need to interview any other advisors. Donna is hired before the meeting ends.

FIRST BROKERAGE OPENS THEIR ACCOUNTS AND INVESTING BEGINS

Donna's assistant, Kent, also supports a few other advisors in the First Brokerage office, and he helps Rick open two identical investment accounts. The first one is for money Donna will manage, and the second one is for money the third-party money manager will supervise. Kent also opens three more accounts: a business account for Rachel's organization service, an IRA for Rick, and another IRA for Rachel.

Up to this point, Rick and Rachel had been keeping all their savings in liquid cash, so it is dispersed and deposited into their new accounts without any trouble (see Table 6.1). Then, Kent sends the approval for the third-party, institutional money manager to begin investing. Donna had described this program with so much admiration that Rick and Rachel feel very comfortable with her personal recommendation.

Table 6.1   Rick and Rachel's Money

Account One	Taxable, jointly owned investment account managed by Donna
Account Two	Taxable, jointly owned investment account with third-party money manager
Account Three	Rachel's business investment account
Account Four	Rick's individual retirement account managed by Donna
Account Five	Rachel's individual retirement account managed by Donna

A few weeks later, Donna calls Rick to explain that the Wall Street money manager is on the job, and she reminds Rick that he can give her a ring whenever it's convenient. Donna adds that she'll soon finish making purchases in that first investment account that she is managing. "She seems willing to answer all our questions," Rick tells Rachel later that night.

Rick remembers from the meeting that Donna said they could expect to see her put their money into a few mutual funds, maybe an annuity, and a few accelerated return notes (ARNs). Rick has almost no experience with investments like these, and he reminds himself that this is partly why they hired her. In fact, Donna does a great job of conveying confidence that her approach will fit their needs because she knows them and the family so well after her analysis of their risk profile questionnaire results.

Since Rachel and Rick are pleased thus far, they don't really dive into the details of their statements right away. Off and on, they get generic sales emails from First Brokerage, which they just delete. After a few months, Kent sends an email asking if they are doing OK. After getting that note, Rachel decides she should carve out some time to look closely at their portfolio. That evening, she and Rick take a few minutes to go through the activity in the accounts by logging in online and checking out what transactions have happened in the portfolio.

They see a few things that don't seem wrong or bad but still feel a little bit surprising. For example, the institutional money manager is doing an extraordinarily large number of transactions every single day in the separately managed account. They had no idea there would be so many orders, and many of them are just for one or two shares of stock at a time. And a lot of it seems repetitive because the institutional Wall Street manager will buy a share or two of a company and then buy or sell a single share of that same company just a few days later.

When looking at the transactions, they found one was a large withdrawal to cover the fee for the third-party money manager. In fact, looking at the date, that fee was the very first thing that happened right after they opened the account! Rick suggests to Rachel that this is probably just standard procedure and nothing to worry about, but neither one of them was prepared for the third-party money manager to take a portion of their savings from their account before doing anything at all for them.

In the investment accounts that Donna manages, they can see that Donna had invested in the annuity and ARNs as they had discussed. It gives them confidence to see that Donna said to expect these investments and then that's what happened. Those investments are in the accounts. Fee-wise, they only see a small, administrative account fee in each account. They share with some other friends about how Donna was giving them good service for just a few dollars per year. "It pays to have a connection in finance," their friends think.

RICK AND RACHEL INQUIRE ABOUT THE THIRD-PARTY MANAGER AND IPOs

Rachel and Rick call Donna to ask about the exorbitant fee charged by the third-party manager, as well as the questionable and seemingly frivolous transactions. "All those transactions they are doing for you prove that they are actively managing your account," Donna explains. "And it's exactly what we hired that manager to do. It's a good thing! Since you filled out that risk profile questionnaire, I am confident every investment you own is suitable to you and your situation."

Rachel notices Donna emphasizing the phrase "suitable to you," and overall, they appreciated Donna's prompt response. As the months turn into years, Donna calls them occasionally to get permission to do a trade in the investment account she supervises. Usually, it's to sell a fund and buy a different, better fund.

At one point, Rick calls Donna concerning a company that is about to be sold for the first time on the stock market. He leaves a voice mail saying, "I'm interested in an initial public offering. Will you help me buy this great company that's going to start trading on the stock market? This isn't an emergency, so please don't feel rushed to call me back, but I read that First Brokerage is underwriting the IPO. I think that means First Brokerage's customers can get shares, so let's be sure to buy some, OK? Looking forward to talking to you more about it. Thanks!"

It takes a few days for her to get back to him, which Rick finds slightly annoying, but since he'd made it clear in his voice mail that it wasn't an emergency, he doesn't address it. When she does finally get back to him, she explains, "I really think there's a lot of risk involved with buying this company in the IPO. It's extremely popular, which means everyone knows about this company and the demand for shares is extraordinarily high. In my experience, it's going to be very difficult to get shares for you at that opening price. But here's the good news. Now that I know you like initial public offerings, I can regularly buy them for you in the future, and we'll definitely be able to get you some shares in the next major IPO that comes along. In fact, right after this popular one, we have another, smaller IPO. How about I commit you for 100 shares?" Rick and Rachel agree, and as the months go by, they participate in many IPOs, but not the one Rick initially called about.

RICK AND RACHEL EXPERIENCE A BAD INVESTMENT AND START TO QUESTION FEES

Time continues to pass, and one Wednesday evening, Rachel is online and notices that her total portfolio value has gone down quite a bit. She asks Rick if he remembers the last time he heard from Donna. He thinks it was when he got a birthday card from her and confirms that he too is surprised about the drop in account value. He tells Rachel that he's been meaning to talk to Donna, because after all this time, the IPO investing doesn't seem to be making a profit.

The very next morning, they call Donna's office, and Kent takes the message like always. Donna takes more than a week to get back to them. Perturbed, Rick explains that they are surprised at how much the accounts have fallen and specifically notes that one of the ARN investments has lost almost 90 percent of its value. Donna shares that she understands their point of view very well, and she gives an excellent description of the risks versus the rewards when using investments like accelerated return notes. Rick can appreciate that there were never any guarantees, and as the conversation comes to an end, Donna offers to sell that ARN. She says, "Since we're selling it for a loss, I'm sure it will lower your tax bill." Rick and Rachel think it sounds good to be able to pay less in taxes, so they give Donna the green light to sell the ARN.

Donna then explains she has another fund that she'll buy using the proceeds from the sale of the ARN. When they hang up, Rick thinks it's odd that she was so quick to buy something new. He wonders why she didn't have to do any homework at all and yet immediately had another investment to buy in place of the ARN. These thoughts lead him to suspect that Donna collected a commission when she first bought the investment for him, she'll earn another one when she sells it, and maybe she'll get a third commission when she buys the next fund she mentioned. Doing some homework online, he learns it's common for clients to only see an administrative charge in a brokerage account because Donna can collect her commission in other ways. Rachel suggests that maybe it would be a good idea to show their portfolio to another advisor and get a second opinion.

RICK AND RACHEL GET A SECOND OPINION AND A SALES PITCH

Rick calls Larry at Second Brokerage after seeing Larry's ad in the community bulletin. Just like First Brokerage, Second Brokerage offers many additional services such as insurance, mortgages, tax advice, and credit cards. Larry agrees to look over their recent statements, and he welcomes Rick and Rachel to his office to go over the findings.

After exchanging pleasantries, Larry says, "I'd like to start with a list of basic bullet points that I think you should be aware of. The first one is that the fees charged by the annuity company are much too high. Additionally, the third-party money manager has lost too much money. Also, the mutual funds your other advisor bought have fees that were charged up front, which could have been avoided. Along those lines, when your other advisor sold the ARN, there was a back-out fee, which means that you've lost almost every cent on that investment."

Rick and Rachel are stunned. Rachel asks, "How do we fix these things?"

Larry launches into a presentation: "The way to fix all these problems is to work with Second Brokerage and let me make the following changes: I'll buy a different, better annuity for you; I'll fire the institutional money manager and bring in a different one with a better track record; and lastly, I'll sell the mutual funds and buy funds with no up-front fees."

Larry also mentions he's shocked that Donna only sends holiday cards and the occasional email. He explains that he likes it when his clients reach out, and he's very open to when his clients ask to come by the office so they can meet with him and go over the accounts. He hopes Rick and Rachel would enjoy doing that as well.

RICK AND RACHEL HAVE THEIR LOYALTY TESTED

After the two of them leave Larry's office, they decide to stay with Donna out of loyalty to her. Plus, Larry's strategy seems pretty similar to Donna's, so it doesn't seem worth the paperwork to change. They decide to talk to Donna and give her a chance to make these fixes herself. So their next step is to get an appointment with her for an important face-to-face conversation.

Unfortunately, before they can arrange a meeting with Donna, they get a startling call from Francine, their CPA. Francine has been doing their taxes for them for years, and she explains that Donna bought a limited partnership in Rachel's individual retirement account (IRA). Because of how limited partnerships are organized, they create extra tax requirements called K-1 documentation. To file their taxes properly, those documents need to be included and reviewed, which means Rick and Rachel will pay a larger amount for their CPA's service.

Francine has more bad news. In addition to paying more for her services, they will also owe more to the IRS this year because of a rule that says people must pay taxes (and maybe penalties) if they make too much income from a limited partnership inside an IRA. The couple are concerned because they thought profit inside an IRA is protected from taxes until the funds are taken out. Since they haven't drawn from their retirement accounts, they are baffled and annoyed. Apparently, the IRS will want payment because the limited partnership investments that Donna bought made enough income that the tax protection inside the IRA is void. This is the last straw.

RICK AND RACHEL MOVE THEIR PORTFOLIO TO SECOND BROKERAGE

Rachel calls Larry at Second Brokerage to request signature documents so she and her husband can stop working with Donna and start working with him. When Rick explains the extra cost from the CPA, Larry says he can help because he will never buy a limited partnership since many of his clients don't like the K-1 forms for the same reason Rick and Rachel don't. What's more, he can restrict the new third-party money manager from ever buying limited partnerships as well. That sounds great to Rick, and after the accounts have moved, both Rachel and Rick are glad that they can call Larry and request a meeting any time they want to hear about what's going on with their money.

Overall, the process to move their portfolio is less convenient than they'd hoped, and they wouldn't have done it if they hadn't been upset. They have to learn new online procedures, and their CPA reminds them that, this year, they will have two sets of tax documents: one from First Brokerage and another set from Second Brokerage. So her tax preparation fee will be a bit higher the next time they file their taxes.

THE COUPLE WONDER WHY THEY OWN CERTAIN INVESTMENTS

After Larry sells all the accelerated return notes and other things that Donna had bought, he invests their money in several investments titled as different kinds of Second Brokerage mutual funds. These are investments like Second Brokerage Growth Fund and Second

Brokerage Technology Fund. Rick likes the Second Brokerage products because it shows Larry really believes in his company's offerings.

But one evening, Rachel shows her husband an article online that highlights how advisors can make more money by ignoring the best investments available and focusing instead on selling their own company's products to clients. They also briefly wonder about what kinds of investments are inside those Second Brokerage funds because they don't want to support enterprises that conflict with their ethics. Since the accounts aren't doing badly, neither of them feels any urgency to address their concerns.

RICK AND RACHEL
STAY LOYAL TO LARRY

A year later, Larry calls Rick to say he no longer works for Second Brokerage. He's changed firms, and now he is a financial advisor at Third Brokerage. Larry suggests Rick and Rachel follow him to Third Brokerage to continue investing together and describes how, in general, things have been changing for the worse over at Second Brokerage. He shares how happy he is to not have to work there anymore.

Because Rick and Rachel are loyal people and they appreciate that Larry proactively changed firms to do better for his clients, they agree to move their accounts. They get a set of documents in the mail and can tell the process is going to be a lot like when they moved from First Brokerage to Second Brokerage. As they finish that process and get settled into the new online system at Third Brokerage, they are surprised, but don't mind too much, that Larry must sell all those special Second Brokerage–branded investments since Third Brokerage can't hold them.

And the whole process begins once again.

HOW DID WALL STREET TAKE ADVANTAGE OF RICK AND RACHEL?

Many investors reading about Rick and Rachel's situation might recognize that Donna wasn't the best fit for them. But *why*, specifically, was she a poor choice? What's more, many readers may have initially agreed that the move from Donna to Larry was a good one, but was it? Lastly, the move to follow Larry to Third Brokerage is fraught with problems. Chapter 7 pulls back the curtain on what really happened—and why it's so good for the Money Magicians and so bad for the rest of us.

7

LEARN TO HEAR WHAT'S NOT BEING SAID

How Conflicts of Interest, Misleading Titles, Confusing Fees, and Brokerage Sales Quotas Force Financial Advisors to Work Against You

L arry, Donna, and the three brokerages where Rick and Rachel held their money have all failed their clients on multiple fronts, and for much of it, neither Larry nor Donna is individually to blame. It's the system. In fact, the majority of advisors are excellent professionals with very good ethics and morals. I'm not describing financial advisors individually. I'm describing a system—the theater in which the magic show happens—that has such pervasive conflicts of interest and low standards of conduct that it creates too much opportunity for misunderstanding and misuse.

The magician on the stage has to work with the limitations of the theater where he's performing, and it's the same for financial advisors working within brokerage houses on Wall Street. The system is not set up well for the client, and that's a result of the structure doing a disservice to the advisor. Let's focus on financial advisors and pull back the curtain on the many flaws they contend with so that these Wall Street manipulations and tricks don't affect you ever again.

FLAW: The system uses semantics to obscure the advisors' responsibilities.

If they are all titled "financial advisor," don't they all do the same thing?

If your advisor works for a nationwide brokerage firm, her proper title is "broker" because she is employed for the purpose of brokering deals, namely selling investments. But you won't see "stockbroker" on any business cards today because Wall Street titles all their salespeople as "financial advisors," "investment consultants," and "wealth management advisors." Regardless of their title, advisors like Donna and Larry officially represent the brokerage company, not the client.

Even though the vast majority of advisors have their hearts in the right place, legally they represent the brokerage firm, and this is one of the reasons the term "broker" is one that professional investment advisors don't want to be called. Instead, Wall Street has learned that the sales are easiest to complete when the professional's title is "advisor" or "consultant." While certain individuals may be truly committed to advising and consulting, the system they work in does not require it. Wall Street's nationwide brokerages encourage and sometimes require their advisors to do product placement and close deals, which isn't evil by itself, but it's important for those of us on Main Street to know that's how the system is set up.

In such a system, it's very difficult for a client to ascertain who is the right fit. What do you see on the business card of a professional who sells only his company's insurance policies? How about a professional who convinces people to buy mutual funds based on their risk profile? How about a professional who will help you use your investments as collateral to get an interest-only mortgage so you can buy a new house? All these people could show some version of "vice president" and "financial advisor" on their card despite the vast difference in product offering and experience.

On Wall Street, titles typically reflect how good the individual is at selling, because the titles are often awarded based on revenue and sales goals. There's very little connection between the service the person provides (life insurance, annuities, financial planning, retirement plans) and his title. This makes it difficult for clients to hire the appropriate professional for their specific needs.

DISILLUSION

It's extremely difficult to know if the advisor you are talking to is an investing expert who's legally required to put your interests first or a professional salesperson who doesn't legally represent you at all.

FLAW: Quotas might be good for brokerages, but they are very bad for clients.

How does putting the advisor's job on the line help clients?

Wall Street does an excellent job of defining what its brokers—its sales force—should produce. The quota is an institutional fixture, and at most firms, failing to meet it means termination for the advisor. A common quota is that a new hire must bring in $10 million to $20 million within two or three years. Advisors who fail to meet the quota get fired, and the accounts they were able to bring in usually stay with the brokerage, but with a different advisor. This system is not at all about the client, and there are a lot of reasons why brokerages should stop firing advisors for failing to meet quotas.

Put yourself in the shoes of a client who hires a new broker that is still trying to meet her quota. She gives you incredibly personalized service because she doesn't have many clients yet. Sadly, she doesn't reach her quota, and after a year or so, she gets fired. The company introduces you to another advisor at that brokerage, and he likely has a completely different approach to service than the woman you originally hired. By firing her, the brokerage forces you into an entirely new service model when you were quite happy with the service as it was. The disruption isn't to your advantage, and it's reasonable to expect that you might be unhappy with the quality of service and interaction given by the new guy replacing her.

But let's change the scenario so that the original broker does make her quota. You, the hypothetical client, are still going to experience a change in the level of service because she won't have the time to keep giving you so much attention now that she has all these other clients. That is because when she met you (as noted above), she had very few clients. But quotas create a race to sign up clients and a unique desperation centered on remaining employed. She had to promise the moon to close the deal and keep her job, and now she simply doesn't have the time to offer that personalized approach she initially promised.

I'm not talking about individual integrity, because lying, cheating, and stealing are never acceptable, and most advisors are very ethical people. It's not an integrity issue when a new advisor offers a lot of special attention to her potential clients because she's worried about keeping her job. For example, if she offers a home visit every quarter to give a client a market update, she probably does this fully intending to continue to keep her commitment. But after she's met her quota and has a lot of other clients, the company doesn't offer any guidance or incentive for continuing that service. This means her clients will endure a shift in the level of attention they receive.

From the advisor's point of view, giving you great service used to make sense because she'd do whatever she could to not lose her job. But now, it's actually *not* in her best interest because she needs to service all the other clients and still do growth activities. What's more, her brokerage likely supports her when she decides to give you less attention because the company wants her focused on growth.

Another unintended result from the pressure created by quotas is that it promotes criminal behavior. Most advisors are good people who would never break the law, and I'm not suggesting they are criminals. Instead, I'm talking about shady characters that an advisor agrees to work with as she tries to meet a quota and stay employed. The systemic truth is that quotas make advisors more susceptible to real criminals who lie and manipulate the professional for a variety of nefarious reasons. Money laundering has long been a serious crime, and a financial advisor under the pressure of losing her job is an easy target for an experienced criminal.

DISILLUSION

The quota serves Wall Street's bottom line and does not benefit the client.

FLAW: Each advisor must represent a variety of different jobs and career disciplines.

Are you really an expert in investing, insurance, credit, taxes, estate planning, and banking?

Americans typically are attracted to professionals who have focused on a particular discipline for their entire career. We call them "experts," and we have sayings like, "Don't be a jack-of-all-trades, master of none." Culturally, we respect the masters who focus on a skill and do that job well whether it's a pilot, a doctor, or a boat maker. Unfortunately, Wall Street doesn't typically create experts to serve Main Street because it seems the skill that brokerages most want advisors to master is how to juggle a lot of very different products.

Wall Street creates and sells an astonishingly large amount of vastly different products—checking accounts, mortgages, credit cards, mutual funds, life insurance, exchange-traded funds, annuities, stocks, long-term care insurance, bonds, and others—and each brokerage needs its advisory force to distribute them. Therefore, the training focus is often on sales skills. Advisors are typically hired because Wall Street believes they have a network and/or a résumé that will enable them to influence people to buy their products. Because of the staggering array of different offerings at each brokerage, their representatives often focus less on the craft of excellent investing and instead concentrate more on the skills of sales and project management.

From another perspective, it's a strange conflict that occurs when an advisor sells mortgages and credit cards right alongside an investment portfolio. Banks, in general, make a living by collecting interest on debt. When you help consumers go into debt, it immediately lowers the customers' net worth and decreases their personal financial stability because of the additional costs that come with the loan. On the other hand, investment houses are supposed to help consumers raise their net worth by investing money and, in general, increase their customers' financial stability. Professionally, these are two very different mindsets with very different approaches to money. At the very least, professional investors who use debt to buy more investments will agree that leverage usually raises risk and increases the volatility of a portfolio.

If the professional you regularly talk to about your portfolio works for a company that encourages her to sell mortgages, life insurance policies, credit cards, long-term care insurance, and home equity lines of credit, then systemically, you must question the depth of the person's skills in each of those disciplines. Even if you believe your representative is truly an expert in all those fields, is it feasible that the company she works for has the best offering in every one of those product lines? Logically, that's very difficult to accept.

In a system where the broker salesperson needs to sell credit cards, mortgages, and insurance policies on top of investments, brokerages often suggest their salespeople manage it all by delegating the more complex tasks. This means the advisor talking to the client delegates the actual investing to someone else (like a third-party money manager). That's when advisors use products and programs owned directly by the brokerage or, in other situations, advisors use outside firms that have a selling contract with their company. In the case of Rick and Rachel, both Donna and Larry engaged a third-party, "elite" money manager to do a portion of the investing.

When a broker hires a third party to do the investing for you, it's usually with an explanation of how special and highly sought after that manager is within the halls of Wall Street. But many things do not pass the commonsense test here. In the story of Rick and Rachel, their financial advisor Larry offered to restrict the investing so the manager would not buy any limited partnerships. That means, in order to comply with Larry's restrictions, the highly sought-after manager could not purchase what he normally buys. But if a client or advisor can put constraints like that on the "genius" money manager, then perhaps that third party is not as special as we're led to believe.

In many industries, it makes sense to separate the person providing customer service and the person doing the work. For example, when you take your car to get fixed at a dealership, you usually talk to a service representative who is your point of contact for the maintenance. The actual work is done by mechanics that you'll never meet. When you order a dinner at a restaurant, you speak to a waitress focused on making sure she knows what you want, and in the kitchen, there's someone else you will never talk to who prepares the meal.

What makes these separations acceptable is that the result—a fixed car or a cheeseburger—is basically the same for everybody. But in the areas of advice and consulting, that separation is not to the client's advantage. When you go to a doctor, do you want the surgeon to do the work himself, or is it just as acceptable if he farms it out to someone you'll never meet? When you visit a lawyer or CPA or almost any other advice-driven service, people want the expert directly involved. Is it OK if, in the courtroom, the attorney representing you is someone you'd never talked to or even met before? How has the public come to accept this kind of separation from Wall Street?

There are a couple of reasons that it's advantageous for Wall Street to separate the investing from the customer service. First, the brokerages need their salespeople to focus on bringing in new clients, which is a different skill than investing. Every hour that an advisor spends on investing is time that investor is not working to close new business. Second, the separation is an excellent foundation for negotiating with unhappy clients. When the client is upset about something, it's a lot easier to say, "I understand and agree. I recommend we fire that money manager. He won't like it, but you're right—heads must roll. I'll start looking for an alternative immediately, because that manager really let us down." In this setup, accountability somehow belongs with the faceless money manager. It's a lot riskier to Wall Street's bottom line if it makes the brokerage salespeople responsible for investing.

What's more, if the advisor is directly responsible, then Wall Street loses the "Wizard of Oz effect," which is achieved by putting an unknown someone behind a curtain at the end of the yellow brick road. Relationships with "special geniuses" are often highlighted as a benefit of being a client of the brokerage. This myth suggests that if clients put their money in that brokerage's accounts, they will have a unique connection to special experts that no one else can access. It's such an easy bubble to burst because there is no guru on the mountaintop.

When a brokerage offers a financial smorgasbord through the same advisor, then the brokerage is systemically forcing that professional away from giving client-focused advice. This is because advice is different from sales. A salesperson has something to sell, and the salesperson will interact with you in a way to show you the importance of buying it right now. In that interaction, the salesperson seeks to create a sense of urgency and explain away your various reasons for not buying. An expert giving advice has knowledge of a great variety of possible paths and, after understanding your individual situation, can suggest a few paths that should reasonably accomplish your goals.

An excellent way to tell the difference is when the salesperson keeps changing the product to fit whatever the customers say they want. It's a lot like a vacuum salesperson who immediately switches the attachments when the prospects say, "I have hard-to-reach places to clean." It's the same vacuum that the professional needs to sell to make a living. It's just altered to make the sale easier by giving the customers the comfortable feeling that the product provides what they say they want. It isn't wrong or immoral to try to give the customers what they want; it's just not a professional advisor giving unbiased, high-quality advice.

In the example, Rick said he didn't want any limited partnerships, and Larry immediately said that he'd put that restriction on the money manager. Sales isn't evil, and Larry isn't a bad guy, but restricting the money manager didn't materially change the offering. That's still the same product. The program is set up to deceive Rick into thinking he left behind his problems with Donna and First Brokerage when, really, the new system still has the same weaknesses. Larry cannot offer to do the investing for Rick because there isn't enough time in the day to be an expert investor and know all the other product types as well.

DISILLUSION

Forcing the advisor to be a jack-of-all-trades, master of none, is not prioritizing the client's experience.

FLAW: Wall Street creates a systemic conflict of interest when it pays its advisors more to sell the company's products.

Is this investment really the best choice for me, or is it what pays the advisor the most?

When a customer walks into a retail shop—whether the store sells clothes, tires, or ice cream—it's reasonable to expect the salesperson to help make it easy for the customer to buy the company's product. The shopping public, in general, knows that the more it spends, the more money the salesperson or waiter could collect in commission or tip. But when the store offers more than one brand, then things typically change. Take, for example, a shoe store that sells a lot of different brands of footwear. It doesn't matter whether the customer buys Nike or Reebok or Adidas, because the salesperson will get the same commission. The company isn't incentivizing its sales force to push one brand over another.

But some stores take this further because they offer their own products alongside a bunch of other similar products. Grocery stores are a perfect example. They often have their own store brand so that customers can have a choice, buying the name-brand food or the less expensive store brand. If you think about where you buy your groceries, you'll probably recognize that the grocery store has one name, and its food items have another.

The key here is that, more often than not, the customers *pay less to buy the store brand* whether they know it's owned by the grocery store or not. The grocery industry has put the customer first. What's more, no sales representative in the grocery store is pushing the store's brand toward clients in an effort to collect oversized commissions. The food industry in general has a culture of giving its best value to customers.

Compare that with Wall Street culture where there's the same grocery-style smorgasbord of products to pick from, but the client gets treated in almost the opposite manner. The brokerage firm does have a salesperson who is pushing the company-branded products because there is a higher payout for doing so. Additionally, the client might not even know those investments are the brokerage's own products. This is a clear conflict of interest, which forces clients to seriously examine every purchase.

This conflict exists in another, more convoluted way because ABC Brokerage might name its products differently to help hide the fact that it's actually the brokerage's product. For example, ABC Brokerage might create and sell Silver Bear mutual funds, and ABC advisors sell Silver Bear investments all the time to clients who aren't aware that Silver Bear investments are owned by ABC Brokerage. In this case, even a savvy client won't have the opportunity to ask the logical question, "Is this really in my best interest?" By and large, advisors are good people with excellent ethics, but it's systemically wrong for the brokerage to influence them with higher payouts on the firm's own products.

Not every major Wall Street brokerage sells its own products. But some of the ones that don't will still do some double-dealing in another way. For example, a major Wall Street firm could completely shut down its own fund operation and then turn to the rest of Wall Street and say, "If you'd like us to sell your products to our customers, you need to pay us." Publicly, the brokerage announces it doesn't have any proprietary products to sell, while behind the scenes, it collects money from other Wall Street firms for the privilege of exposure to that brokerage's client list.

Some brokerages call this "open architecture," which is a term hinting that the client's advisor can pick any product out there. But the truth is that other Money Magicians are paying the brokerage firm with kickbacks so that their products can be made available to that firm's customers. This is usually the reality behind stock statements like, "Through us and our relationships, you'll get attention from the best money managers that normally you could never have access to." The phrase "our relationships" is code for "They pay us to tell you about them. This isn't us bringing you what's best out there. It's us using you as a product and collecting fees from both sides of the transaction. It's wonderful for our brokerage because the clients pay us to buy the product and the product's makers pay us to provide it to the clients."

Whenever the salesperson or the brokerage firm collects more fees to sell the company's products (whether made by the company or offered through the company), then we're right back to square one where the customers must worry, systemically, if the investment is truly in their best interest or not. Most of my life I've been a financial advisor, and I'm convinced that the preponderance of advisors out there today are extremely ethical, caring people. This isn't about the individual's morality; it's about the fact that the brokerage is set up so that it's impossible for the client to know what is truly motivating the advisor. Maybe the investment the advisor recommends is the right thing at the right price for you. Or maybe the advisor just wants to collect a larger commission. Perhaps the advisor requires a little extra money right now and is pushing an investment to collect the extra pay.

DISILLUSION

The system isn't designed to give the client clarity on what the advisor is trying to accomplish. Maybe it's good investing for the client, or it could just be lining the advisor's pockets. Of course, it could also be a little bit of both.

FLAW: Charging clients up front needlessly hurts their financial picture.

How long is my money actually working for me?
A client paying before any service has been provided is not bad all by itself. There are plenty of consumer situations where customers pay at the start of the engagement. A fast-food restaurant, Amazon

shopping, and tickets to a concert are great examples. But in each of those scenarios, there's a reason the client pays first, and it's central to the value proposition being provided to the client. We pay first for a fast-food hamburger because speed is an important part of the offering. Amazon is also focused on speed and convenience. Pay for the product and quickly get it at your door in a day or two. To attend any concert, it's natural that you pay for the tickets long before you get to see the show.

When Wall Street charges clients matters, and it's usually right at the start. That's important because the timing of the payments determines how long your money is in your account working for you. Let's say you put $100 in an account and on the first day $5 is removed to pay the brokerage. You start out with just $95. Compare that to someone who doesn't pay Wall Street's fee until *after* one full month or a calendar quarter has passed. The second person has more of his money working for him more of the time.

The main reason Main Street hires Wall Street is to help Main Street grow its portfolios, and an easy, mathematically sound way of doing that is to charge *after* the work is done. Wall Street collecting its fee up front is as good a proof as any that its main objective is to increase its own wealth, *not* that of its clients. This is the opposite of a client benefit, because at the nationwide brokerage level, collecting all those fees on all those accounts up front equals really big money. That really big money should stay with the clients.

That up-front fee means those funds stop working for you as soon as they are removed, and this isn't a mandatory requirement. There are investment advisory firms that charge *in arrears*, meaning after the work is done. Financial advisors, in general, are not trying to worsen your wallet, but the system forces them to do so every time the brokerage collects at the start of the engagement. Up-front fees are an unnecessary disadvantage to the client, and it clearly goes against the very thing Wall Street supposedly offers.

DISILLUSION

Over time and a lot of disadvantaged clients, it's extremely profitable for the brokerage to collect fees up front, and that's exactly what happens.

FLAW: It's systemically inappropriate to charge clients a back-out fee.

Wait a second—are you saying I have to pay you to get my own money?

The back-out fee is a common method that brokerages use to collect money from their clients. It is the fee clients must pay to get their own money out of an investment product they recently bought. Usually, products with a back-out fee also have ongoing internal fees to cover the operating costs of making the product exist and function.

As already described, one of the ways the system pays a financial advisor is by collecting a commission right at the start when the sale is first entered. Sometimes, the salesperson gets a commission from the financial institution that made the product, so the client isn't even aware that a fee was paid. That's where the back-out fee is born. The investment company paid a salesperson a bunch of money in the form of an up-front commission, so now the company can't let the client have her money back until enough time has passed for the company's ongoing operating costs to recoup that initial payout that it gave the advisor.

But it doesn't have to be this way. Plenty of industries pay salespeople, and then, if the sale really isn't final and the customers want their money back, the salesperson returns the commission (or gets less commission going forward). Somehow, Wall Street has convinced its clientele that when the salesperson fails to convince them to hold onto the investments they purchased, it's the *clients* who have to pay.

The Money Magicians will sweeten the pot by making the commission quite large in the hope of attracting more brokers to push their product toward clients. A good salesperson can make a lot of money in this arrangement, but the system is manipulating the advisors to sell these products. It's not the financial advisors' fault that the system influences them to consider higher payouts from certain investments. Nor are they to blame for the brokerage firm charging clients the back-out fee when the customers decide they'd like to sell their investment. But clearly none of this is in the client's best interest.

DISILLUSION

The broker who received the sales commission should pay the back-out fees when their customers want their money back, but instead, Wall Street charges Main Street.

FLAW: Brokerages force advisors to use their own customers as products.

What's in it for me, the customer, to have to change investment companies?

When Larry moved from Second Brokerage to Third Brokerage, he asked Rick and Rachel to move with him. What actually was going on behind the curtain? The brokerage-to-brokerage move happens quite frequently. When a financial advisor leaves one brokerage to go to another one, the rest of the world thinks that it's just like when any employee decides to leave a company for a new job across the street. But it's actually very different because most brokerages (certainly all the major ones) pay the financial advisor to make the move.

When an advisor collects compensation to move brokerages, it's often a sizable amount of money, and it isn't simply a payment to make the transition. An advisor with an average-sized practice can easily earn six- and seven-digit payouts to successfully change firms. But many strings are often attached. The most common one: the advisor has a short period of time in which to bring over the majority of her clients; otherwise she cannot keep the money.

From the brokerage's point of view, it needs to attract financial advisors who have paying clients so that the firm can cash in on the revenue those clients generate. When the brokerage convinces an advisor to jump ship and move to its firm, the system is set up so that the brokerage can't lose. If the advisor brings over the clients, the brokerage and advisor both win. If the advisor cannot convince her clients to follow her in time to keep her bonus, the brokerage still wins because the advisor has to return the bonus. So the advisor can lose, but only if she is bad at sales and doesn't have loyal clients.

Sadly, the clients almost always lose because they must either deal with a new financial advisor if they don't move to the new firm or contend with new account numbers, new online credentials, and new restrictions at a different firm. One of the most common restrictions when clients agree to move firms relates to which investments can move with them. Often, certain investments cannot move to the new firm, and the customer is forced to sell these holdings, which is a disservice to the client for a number of reasons. The main reason is that these transactions didn't occur in connection with the client's needs. The sales had no basis in how the investments were doing in the markets. Instead, the sales were based on the timing of their advisor's career move. Another reason these transactions are a disservice is because clients might have to pay taxes or back-out fees that they otherwise wouldn't have to pay. The system pressures advisors to look the other way while trying to "close the deal" so they can keep that big bonus connected to a successful move to the new firm.

From the advisor's point of view, jumping from brokerage to brokerage every few years is an excellent way to collect extra compensation. It's important to note that there are a lot of high-integrity advisors out there, so of course there's some validity when they call a client and say, "I changed firms to give you something better."

However, these payouts are often seven digits. That systemically forces the public to wonder, "Is this move really in the best interest of the client, or does the advisor just want to earn and keep a massive payout?"

Closing all one's accounts and moving to another brokerage firm to stay with the same advisor is often not in a client's best interest. As a small matter, there's the simple inconvenience of it all. Then, consider the promise that the clients will be getting something better if they move. The financial industry is highly regulated, and it's extremely difficult to find a measurable and material difference between the major brokerages today. *How* will it be better besides the fact that your advisor can get rich using the client as a commodity? What if Wall Street prominently disclosed that its newly hired advisor just received over a million dollars but can't keep that money unless he transfers the majority of his clientele within three to six months? Suddenly, you might not feel so willing to move over to the new firm.

Another problem a client should think about before changing firms is that the advisor must undergo a steep learning curve. The new firm has different software and different people providing various support. For the advisor, that means almost everything is going to be operationally new. All these little differences take time to get used to, which means mistakes are more probable in the first six to twelve months.

If Wall Street really wanted what's best for the client, there would be some grace period to permit the new advisor time to get used to the new systems and culture. Wall Street wouldn't apply the quota starting the first day, and instead it would give advisors an opportunity to complete training and get accustomed to the new office. But what happens is that as soon as the Larries of the world quit Second Brokerage, they immediately reach out to their clients to convince them to move to Third Brokerage. This means that Wall Street's system forces advisors to use their most loyal clients as part of their on-the-job training, so the advisors can get accustomed to the new way of doing things with the loyal customers who moved first and won't complain.

Whenever an investment transaction occurs as a result of an advisor changing firms, the Money Magicians just performed another trick. Buying and selling investments should be directly connected to the client's goals and the current market environment. But when advisors recommend transactions solely connected to the logistics of moving the account to the new firm, the actual stock market and investing environment is not the catalyst. The client's needs and goals have nothing to do with those purchases or sales.

This is also an injustice because there are thousands and thousands of investments that can move to any brokerage without fees or other restrictions. It's easily possible for anyone to have a top-tier portfolio without buying things that can only be held in one brokerage account. What's more, the rules making those investments immobile are not laws or client-focused benefits. They are just protectionist policies created by the brokerage to help make it difficult for clients to leave.

Transactions connected to brokerage-to-brokerage moves raise serious ethical questions. Clearly, this is not about serving the client, nor is it even remotely to the client's advantage. But the financial advisor's pocketbook gets fatter. The new Wall Street brokerage now gets to collect additional fees from all the new clients opening up accounts. This backward environment plainly works for the Money Magicians instead of their clients.

The main reason investors follow their broker, despite all the disadvantages, is because they like their advisor personally. The Money Magicians rely heavily on client emotion, and advisors often offer their friendship as an important reason to work together. This isn't bad by itself. When you know, like, and trust your financial advisor, it really makes for a productive and prosperous business relationship. But when your advisor collects a payout on the condition that he can convince you to follow him to his new firm, it's logical to question how much he returns your loyalty.

DISILLUSION

A major payment to advisors contingent on moving their clientele turns each customer into a product, and that's no way to treat a friend.

8

LEARN TO SEE WHAT'S BEING HIDDEN

How Undefined Service Offerings, Low Legal Standards, an Inappropriate Consolidation of Authority, and Conflicts of Interest Allow Brokerages to Influence and Overrule Clients

B efore I put out my own shingle, I spent 12 years as a financial advisor at one of the large, globally known brokerage firms. When it came to growing my clientele and assets under management, I did better than being in the top 5 percent or even in the top 1 percent of all the advisors in the entire company; by some measurements, I was in the top fraction of 1 percent. It was common in those days for the company's leaders to ask leading financial advisors to publicly share our methods so others could try to do it as well. At one of those elite conferences in New York City, I stood alongside other select top performers behind a podium to offer my "secret sauce for growth." From that banquet hall stage in a swanky Manhattan hotel, I spoke to a room of about 200 office managers. Those managers hoped to take our ideas back to their offices around the country and share them with the salespeople they supervised.

Before my three-to-five minutes were up, I was heckled off the stage.

When it comes to sales methods, people want the quick answer—the technique, the tactic, the touch. But my message wasn't one out of a Hollywood movie starring Michael Douglas. "We have to put the client first," I said. "The practices in the brokerage as a whole need to commit to the person we are advising before the needs of the firm."

You could hear the disappointment as the members of the audience stirred in their seats. I went on with ideas about removing conflicts of interest and setting a firmwide service standard that clients could rely upon. I'll never forget the voice that called out, almost angrily, "You want me to tell advisors how to serve their clients? My job is to tell them about the results we need to accomplish. They can service the clients however they want to achieve those goals."

As I tried to continue, the stage lights feeling hotter now, another Wall Street manager yelled out, "Don't tell me how to do my job! Tell me what you've done to get so many clients so fast."

I exited the stage to boos and exclamations, one being, "I'm not a micromanager!"

They asked what worked for me. I told them. They didn't want to listen. It was one of the galvanizing moments that led me to write this book.

Wall Street's policies and procedures at the brokerage level create industry norms that, even under the best interpretations, can easily be described as detrimental to clients. As discussed in prior chapters, where a magician's theater has trap doors, mirrors, and hidden compartments, the brokerage house has extremely low legal standards, a complete absence of client service models, and a variety of serious conflicts of interest. The playing field is significantly tilted against Main Street in favor of Wall Street's brokerage firms. In the previous chapter, we discussed the biggest flaws at the advisor level. With an understanding that a firm's culture and practices strongly influence the advisor, let's now examine some of the biggest flaws at the brokerage level so that these illusions can't ever claim you as a victim.

FLAW: No major Wall Street brokerage has a firmwide customer service model.

If I hire you, how are you going to take care of me and keep me informed?

At first glance, it seems hard to accept that there's no customer service policy of any kind on Wall Street that applies equally to all advisors. Main Street simply cannot rely on a well-defined, base level of service. In other industries, companies often have policies for how to engage with customers and keep them informed, so it seems to go without saying that the financial sector would as well. Some specific companies set admirable customer service standards such as the premier lodging firm, Ritz Carlton. The company's website highlights its "Gold Standards," which include specific "Steps of Service" and "Service Values." For example, leaders at Ritz Carlton require their staff to warmly greet guests in very specific ways.

Companies from all industries work hard to become well known for high customer service standards because excellent service empowers the client. If the service provider and the service recipient both clearly know what the standard is, then when it's not met, the customer can easily understand and communicate that. This means the company has better opportunities to address the problem. Without a clear and shared expectation of the service, one might say the client is just complaining because he didn't get what he wanted. Businesses standardize basic client interactions for their employees so that customers and staff can both enjoy the comfort of understanding the minimum expectations.

This does not exist at any major brokerage in America. And it's by design.

When you sign the papers to hire a financial advisor at a brokerage firm, the fact is, you don't know when or if you're going to hear from the advisor. Some advisors call their biggest clients every month and their smallest clients once a year. Other advisors choose to never call their clients, preferring instead to rely on emails and newsletters. A third group of advisors likes to send birthday and holiday cards, and if they hear of a major family event, they will send a present. Some other advisors only call clients based on what they hear in the market, meaning they will call their clients when something pops up in the news that could help with a sale (and a commission).

Why is it set up this way? As we saw with Rick and Rachel, brokerages do not define service at the firmwide level because the client is not really their focus. The broker working for the brokerage is the true driving force of revenue; therefore, Wall Street caters to the advisors by giving them carte blanche to handle customer service however they see fit (as long as they bring in the money). As my heckler in New York City said, "I'm not a micromanager!" Wall Street's refusal to hold all their brokers to a clear, minimum standard of outreach means that there are a lot of advisors who simply don't offer good customer service because it's not required of them.

DISILLUSION

The statement "I haven't heard from my advisor" is ubiquitous because the Money Magicians set standards for growth instead of customer outreach.

FLAW: No service model means no accountability.

How can I ensure my financial advisor keeps me informed?

Without a clear definition of service, advisors will often task the client with maintaining the communication in their professional relationship: "If you need something, just call me." With this approach, clients pay a fee to an advisor, and yet they still bear the burden of reaching out and scheduling a review of the portfolio. It's one thing for a client to think of a question and call the advisor. It's another thing altogether for the client to be obligated to initiate regular, repeating service requirements that could have been predicted by the advisor and the brokerage. Things like an annual review of the portfolio or a regular checkup on account beneficiaries shouldn't be the client's responsibility to initiate.

Technology backed by powerful software and artificial intelligence helps advisors to camouflage their lack of service. Today, mass emails, risk profile questionnaires, cookie-cutter portfolios, and regular newsletters make it seem like the advisor is doing a lot of community outreach when, in fact, the automated nature of it is an illusion of customer service. The reality is that those clients still bear the burden of touching base with an advisor that doesn't know them well. Sending people AI-generated, generic emails on a regular basis is typically not recognized as top-notch customer service. In most circles, that's called spam or junk mail.

Accountability to the client gets muddier and muddier as there are more and more people or companies involved in the service. If a client is paying an advisor, a brokerage, and a third-party money manager for investment advice, then who's really responsible for the money and for keeping the customer informed? Systemically, they are all taking fees from the portfolio, and probably at a rate higher than average. By using a structure that involves all these parties, Wall Street makes it very difficult for a client to hold them accountable.

Typically, if you feel you're making money, then the advisor is successful. If you don't feel that way, then the advisor just fires some faceless, third-party money manager and is still successful. Without any clear standard for advisor outreach, we're left looking at the performance of the portfolio. The dirty secret of Wall Street is that no one can predict the future, and if clients strictly compared their portfolio's gains with the S&P 500, they'd have to fire their advisor on a very regular basis because the stock market moves unpredictably in patterns that take years to unfold. This means that as the years turn into decades, even the best money managers face the truth that no investment advisor always makes profits without ever losing. Similarly, there is no money manager who always beats the indexes. Strict clients will have to find a new advisor every few years, or they could pull back the curtain and demand the Money Magicians commit to a clear, easy-to-understand service model.

If an advisor is required by her company to commit in writing to calling every client, every quarter, that's easy to measure. When a client doesn't hear from his advisor for half a year, then it's obvious the service isn't happening. The client could report his situation to a manager, who then could hold the advisor accountable by refunding fees or assigning a new advisor who adheres to the firm's service policy.

The point is that business relationships require interaction to exist. No interaction, or inappropriate interaction, means the relationship is failing and the customer is not properly informed. The Money Magicians keep their advisors happy at the expense of clients by not instituting and enforcing a minimum standard describing that interaction. It all adds up to making it very difficult for clients to know what they are getting for the fees they are paying.

DISILLUSION

If you don't know when your advisor will be personally reaching out to you again, then you don't have a service standard in place.

FLAW: Low legal standards align brokerages against the client.

Whom does the financial advisor legally represent?

The biggest systemic illusion performed by Wall Street involves the vast difference between what brokerages legally must offer and what clients assume they are receiving. Customers like Rick and Rachel think Wall Street is giving them investment advice that is in their best interest. Such investment advice is legally known as a "fiduciary standard." But the reality is that most of the Wall Street brokerage systems require only that investment advice given to customers be *suitable* to each client's situation, meaning the investment matches the results of the risk profile questionnaire.

It doesn't matter how expensive the investment is or whether there are similar, better investments out there. Donna, the financial advisor, told Rick and Rachel that their investments were suitable, meaning the securities could have been the most expensive possible investments available, but they were in line with the client's official profile. These two different standards, *suitable* and *fiduciary*, are at the heart of many of the problems clients have with the Money Magicians.

Legally, the *suitable* standard does not require that the advisor or the investment firm put the client's best interest first. Brokerages, for the most part, prefer to operate under the inadequate *suitable* standard because it permits their sales force to recommend investments that have extremely high fees even though a similar investment could be found with lower costs. In some cases, the advisor might look at several ways of selling the exact same mutual fund. Each method of sale operates under a different ticker symbol on the stock exchange but represents the same underlying fund. The only difference is cost. They are the same fund from the same investment company, all run by the same manager. They are basically all the same investment, but they have different ticker symbols because each product charges the client a different amount.

Under the *suitable* standard, it's acceptable for the advisor to sell the most expensive share class and collect the most exorbitant fee as long as that fund is in the right category as defined by the risk profile questionnaire. For example, if I answered the 10 to 20 questions that usually make up a firm's risk profile questionnaire, I might be categorized as Aggressive, while my wife would probably be Moderate. There are typically seven categories with names like "Extremely Conservative," "Conservative," "Moderately Conservative," "Moderate," "Moderately Aggressive," "Aggressive," and "Extremely Aggressive."

The questions typically focus on your feelings about investing coupled with some basic facts about your life and investment experience. The reason my wife would be categorized differently from me is because she *feels* differently about investing and her answers to the questions would be different. For example, here's a normal kind of question found on a risk profile questionnaire: "If you invest $1 million, how much is an acceptable loss? (A) $0; (B) $100,000; (C) $250,000; (D) $500,000; and (E) All of it." When she answers this question, she is giving the company insight into how she *feels* about investing. She and I have shared a life together for over 20 years, so our monetary situation is the same. That means our separate categories represent the difference in our comfort level with risk and loss.

While people get labeled with a single category, most investments have blurred lines and can be said to fall into two or three different categories. This makes it very hard to hold the Money Magicians accountable for something unsuitable unless the advisor makes an egregious mismatch between the investments and the assigned category. All this adds up to the *suitable* standard being great for the brokerage, not the client.

For years, the brokerages have resisted raising this legal standard, and the latest failed attempt to remove *suitable* investing is called Regulation Best Interest. After years of debate, the watered-down rule that was enacted on June 30, 2020, still allows suitable investing for clients like Rick and Rachel because they have a business account. Further, it only requires advisors consider their clients' best interests at the time of sale as opposed to always putting the client's needs first.

In a perfect world, professional athletes never cheat, and rock stars all write and sing their own songs, but real life teaches us otherwise. It's the same as assuming your advisor is working under a fiduciary standard. People mistakenly believe that their advisor is legally required to put their best interest above the firm's desire to make more money. In that perfect world, the investment expert working for the brokerage house would choose the least expensive route almost every time. But that doesn't happen.

There is an important legal difference between the *suitable* and *fiduciary* standards, which would be obvious in a court of law. To see that difference, clients don't have to be experts on the various investor profiles or know what investments fit into which profiles. Customers just need to know this simple reality: When you find out your representative at the brokerage could have sold you a similar investment for less than you paid, then you are not dealing with a fiduciary. Neither the representative nor the brokerage is acting in your best interest, and you cannot hold either of them meaningfully accountable for not representing you to the best of their ability.

In everyday life, there's almost no way to tell which standard an investment firm enforces on its sales force. From an outsider's perspective, whether or not the brokerage is systemically required to put the client's best interest first is largely hidden from view. When Rick and Rachel met Donna and later spoke with Larry, they didn't know that, legally, both of those financial advisors could sell them investments that did not support their best interests. The first, second, and third brokerage firms in the example offer *suitable* investments, which means the financial recommendations don't have to represent the best efforts of the advisor to find the best financial products.

The *suitable* standard creates several problems and serious conflicts of interest. By firing Donna and hiring Larry, Rachel and Rick thought they had improved their situation when in actuality both Donna and Larry work in the same system under the same rules. Those rules state that Donna and Larry can act in a way that puts their brokerage's interest ahead of the client. Those rules state that Donna and Larry can earn more money, win vacations, or display lofty titles on their business cards if they sell certain things the brokerage wants sold.

I know firsthand there are a lot of ethical, kind, hardworking financial advisors out there. I'm describing the system where the client comes second as a matter of structure. Let's pretend Larry's new firm, Third Brokerage, rolls out an incentive plan to send Larry to the Bahamas for vacation. All Larry has to do is sell a certain amount of Third Brokerage mutual funds. This is not illegal or evil. It's actually pretty common in the realm of sales, but it certainly raises the question of what's ethical. If Larry calls Rick and Rachel to offer a fund owned by Third Brokerage, shouldn't they be aware that Larry might be thinking about earning a vacation instead of wanting to help them achieve their goals?

DISILLUSION

Clients must pay a lot more attention to their money at a brokerage that legally commits to the mediocre standard of providing *suitable* investment advice.

FLAW: A risk profile questionnaire is not enough for a brokerage that truly puts the client's needs first.

I'm comfortable with certain investments, but are they really the ones that will help me accomplish my goals?

Sadly, brokerage salespeople don't have to know their customers that well because legally, the *suitability* standard makes it unnecessary to deeply connect with the clients. Operationally, brokerages offer cookie-cutter investment models to help ensure advisors don't have to spend the time on personalized investment-oriented activities.

Instead of doing all the work that goes into providing individualized investment offerings, they can stay focused on growth-oriented activities. Typically, the advisor gives clients a risk profile questionnaire, determines how they feel about investing, and then puts them into a standardized portfolio along with everyone else who answered those 10 multiple-choice questions in a similar way.

When Rick and Rachel filled out their risk profile questionnaire, their categories became the basis for deciding which investments were *suitable* to them. But because those questionnaires focus so much on how individuals *feel* about investing, they also become powerful sales tools. From the brokerage's point of view, the sales process moves along much smoother when customers feel good about what they are buying. But are customers' feelings truly that important in determining the proper investments?

In any other meaningful endeavor, people begin with the end in mind, and they do the things that will accomplish their goals *in spite of* how they feel. For example, if I'm not feeling well, I go to the doctor. Once it's clear I am ill, I undergo treatment. I didn't want to do any of those things, but my comfort with the medicine is irrelevant next to the goal of getting better. If I want to buy a car, it's normal for the salesman to ask what I enjoy driving because that could help him sell me a car. But my love of convertible sports cars has no bearing on my need for a van to safely haul my six-person family around.

Imagine if a football player said, "I know the goal is to train hard so we can win the game, but I'm really comfortable getting a tan on the beach, so we're going to have to include a fair amount of that." All the parents reading this book have had to redirect their kids away from what's comfortable and *feels* good (playing video games, eating candy, playing with the light socket) so their children will engage in what is needed and *is* good (studying, eating vegetables, playing with toys).

Wall Street has taught the members of the investing public that if they buy investments that *feel* appropriate, then they are doing something right. The risk profile questionnaire is a regulatory requirement across the industry for every client, but what about when people's goals require that they invest outside their comfort zone? For instance, imagine a couple who are really scared of taking risk, but the path they need to walk requires that they invest aggressively. In this scenario, the couple needs to take uncomfortable risks in order to accomplish their goals.

But I've found the opposite scenario to be much more common. When a couple has taken risks all their lives, it's normal that they'd get comfortable continuing with those risky investments. They *feel* like the right thing to do is participate in oversized risk because that's what has led to their success so far. But at this point in their life, they need to be comfortable with *less risk* because they are older, and with a good-sized nest egg, they don't need to put it at risk any longer. The thing that feels comfortable no longer supports their goals, but they don't know that yet.

DISILLUSION

The risk profile questionnaire, by itself, often points people toward investments that serve their feelings over their actual goals.

FLAW: Brokerage firms produce their own investment statements.

Didn't we learn anything from Bernie Madoff?

When Bernie Madoff was caught running one of the biggest Ponzi schemes in history, there was a serious lesson to be had. The cornerstone in the arch of Madoff's plots was the fact that he had two different authorities centralized under one roof. He had authority over the money itself, giving him trading and transfer capability. He also had authority over creating the statements that gave him power over what his clients saw to be true about their portfolio (perhaps this is a good time to go back to Chapter 4 where we discuss how the only way to *see* an investment is through the statement). If Madoff had operated under a system that divided these powers, that Ponzi scheme would have been impossible to achieve.

Who doesn't appreciate the importance of checks and balances and the separation of power? Whether it's a question of church and state or the three branches of America's federal government, there's systemic strength in certain divisions of power. This is why auditing firms exist. No one takes the financials of a company seriously unless an unbiased third party takes a look at them. Without an audit from an objective outsider, there really isn't any financial report worth considering.

Yet if you keep your money at a major brokerage firm, you will be looking at statements that the brokerage itself produced. The Wall Street brokerage has the same two powers as Bernie Madoff because it can manage your money and also create the statement that describes your portfolio to you. This is a serious systemic weakness because this structure makes it easier to send out fake (or inaccurate) statements to clients. I'm not suggesting that large, national brokerage firms are sending out false statements. I'm saying that's too much power in one place, and it's bound to lead to scandal and crime.

DISILLUSION

Combining the powers of managing and reporting on your portfolio is an unnecessary vulnerability and a serious systemic flaw.

FLAW: Wall Street brokerages create false value through the fabrication of exclusivity.

How much money do I really need in order to work with you?
The employees in the majority of "special" Wall Street firms are just businesspeople trying to make money like everyone else. The unique relationship between the brokerage company and its third-party investment firms is simply a contract where the brokerage charges the fund manager to access the brokerage's salespeople and their customer base. Once again, regular investors on Main Street are the product instead of the client.

Often, these "special" Wall Street firms use a very powerful method to create interest in their products and services: exclusivity. You must know the right person with the right relationships; otherwise, you can't have access. But it's important to remember that exclusivity is not, in itself, excellence. It just means that a lot of people can't get it. Phrases like "forbidden fruit" and terms like "FOMO" remind us that we can be deeply affected by the simple statement, "You can't have what I have." We saw in Chapter 5 how natural it is for people to hurt their own progress just to ensure someone else doesn't get an unfair advantage. Exclusivity alone doesn't make a thing valuable, but the human condition gets satisfaction in having something that others cannot.

One way to pierce this veil of exclusivity is to examine *when* the manager purchases investments. The supposed experts at third-party money managers are often required to invest almost all your money as soon as you make the deposit. That means that as your funds come in, they get immediately invested according to that manager's program rules. Does anyone believe that the right time to buy is always right at that moment you happen to make a deposit? How is that top-tier money management?

In my own career, I've found that clients get their biggest bonuses and have the most extra money when the market is flying high. That means that when things are going well and investments cost a lot to buy, it's also when people tend to have extra money. What's more, since things are going well in the economy, it feels comfortable for clients to buy investments at that time, but it's reasonable to pause for a moment. Do you really want to purchase while things are expensive? Perhaps it's wise to look around before investing, because a little patience could give you a buying opportunity in the near future. Unfortunately, most third-party, institutional money managers are required, systemically, to immediately put all deposits to work. That's not putting the client first. That's a cookie-cutter, one-size-fits-all approach that will never substitute for top-notch customer service.

Another method to create the illusion of value is when the sense of exclusivity is created using money itself. If you don't have the money, you can't get into the VIP area. This twist throws away the relationship. Now, you don't have to know anyone special. But you do have to have $10 million to play.

One of my clients owns an insurance practice, and he insures bars and nightclubs. He shared with me once that the easiest way to influence people is to "put up a rope." In the cold light of day, the club is a square room with nothing to differentiate the experience in one corner or the other. But when the club puts up a red velvet rope separating one corner from the rest of the room, it changes everything. People can't help but look at the "special" people in the VIP section and wonder how to get the thing they can't have (all because of a fabricated exclusivity created by a little red rope). Wall Street does the same thing, but not with a rope. Instead, it artificially inflates a salesperson's status by pretending a certain amount of money is required to work with that financial advisor. Almost everyone has heard an investment professional snootily announce, "I only work with people who have [fill-in-the-blank] dollars."

I've traveled the country and spoken with thousands of advisors and seen this truth: They *aim* to work with people who invest a certain amount. That's different from genuinely being unable or unwilling to work with less money. This imaginary line in the sand creates a false exclusivity. For example, financial salespeople often say that a client must have $1 million to work with them. But if you could secretly examine the list of clients for one of those advisors hiding up in a supposedly exclusive ivory tower, you'd find that the advisor has plenty of clients below the stated minimum.

There are several basic, real-life reasons that this line in the sand is as fake as the red rope in the nightclub. For example, the advisor's biggest client has a cousin who doesn't have much money, but the advisor takes on the cousin's accounts anyway to avoid offending her most lucrative client. Or the advisor works with a client who has a little bit more than the line in the sand requires, and after some bad investments, the account is now worth half of that. A final example is whenever the advisor believes the client will soon have a lot of money. It's a very rare brokerage salesperson who would say, "Sorry, I don't have time for you. You see, you are in the process of selling your mega yacht, so you don't actually have the money yet. Don't talk to me until the boat sells."

There's another reason the line in the sand isn't real. Things change. When an advisor starts her career, she needs any client she can find in order to meet her quota and earn a living. But a few years later, she can be more selective. As time passes, an advisor's clientele changes. I remember a Wall Street sales trainer who told a lot of advisors, "Every investment professional should create and publicize one's minimum account size because exclusivity is influence. The best way to approach what that minimum amount should be is to look at your overall list of clients each year. Do the quick math to determine your average account size. Make that average account size your minimum. Don't accept anything below that average, and then, the following year, look at your list of clients again. Do the calculation again, and you'll find that your average account size has grown. Repeat until rich!"

DISILLUSION

The folks on Wall Street use false exclusivity to make you desire them. But the simple truth is that they are privileged to work with you. Not the other way around.

FLAW: Brokerages use the pay-to-play approach to initial public offerings.

Why can't I get shares of that hot new company coming out next month?

Another example of Wall Street tricking clients into paying to be the product occurs when people want to buy initial public offerings. When most private companies want to go public, they have a reputation problem—namely, they don't have one. The vast majority of the private companies seeking to sell themselves to the public don't have any notoriety or fame. Since they aren't celebrity companies, people, in general, have never heard of them, which makes it harder for Wall Street to sell ownership in them. Over the years, the brokerage houses have figured out a way to get around that.

Wall Street's investment bankers charge money for the service of creating that reputation. Among other things, the investment bankers create a "package," or story, that will help make it easy for the sales force of financial advisors to influence clients who otherwise would never have learned of the company's existence. The problem for Wall Street is that this, by itself, is still not enough. That's where celebrity companies come in.

Every once in a while, a company will go public that does have some celebrity status (consider Tesla, Visa, and Facebook, which were all household names before going public). These rare, famous companies already have a lot of attention, and many people know about them, and in general, the public wants to buy shares. When those rare, high-profile IPOs come around, Wall Street uses them to entice their customers into buying the other, less popular IPOs that the brokerage is working to sell. The way brokerages entice clients looks similar to what happened to Rick in Chapter 6. Clients must participate regularly in every unknown IPO the brokerage offers in order to gain access and participate in the next well-known IPO.

Most people see the system the same way Rick and Rachel did. They heard about an IPO that they wanted, and they saw that their advisor's brokerage was helping to bring that company public. So they called their advisor to get involved, thinking they'd be able to get shares. But they were refused those shares (in a very gentle but polite way that was, nevertheless, a policy-driven rejection). The reason is not because their advisor Donna was a bad person. It's because the system is set up to turn Rick and Rachel into a commodity that the brokerage firm can sell.

In this system, Rick and Rachel aren't even the client. The real customers are the various private companies that pay Wall Street to sell their company to the public. The Money Magicians collect fees on both sides of that transaction, because investment bankers get fees from the private companies to bring them public while the individual clients pay fees or commissions when they buy those new shares. Everyone involved in the process pays Wall Street from all sides.

You, the individual customer, will not be allowed to select an occasional IPO to buy if you only want to buy the popular ones. To be good at bringing an unknown company public, Wall Street makes IPOs into a kind of subscription service where regular clients have to buy almost every IPO that the brokerage brings public if they want "the next big one." That means the Money Magicians use people's desire to get involved with the occasional, popular IPO to make money by offering up other, unknown companies to the public.

DISILLUSION

Wall Street's pay-to-play IPO system ensures that most clients cannot invest in the occasional IPO that they actually want.

FLAW: When the brokerage offers investment advice *and* tax filing services, a conflict of interest is created.

When I buy certain investments, will it increase the cost of my tax return?

A straightforward conflict of interest rarely discussed on Wall Street is the combination of tax services and investment advice under the same roof. Typically, each service would be performed by two different professionals in two different departments at the same company. Occasionally though, it could be the same person who works as a tax advisor and also sells investments for a living. Either way, there's a systemic conflict of interest that occurs when the firm charges separately for the investment services and the tax preparation services.

The financial advisor collects investment fees (see Appendix A for a more in-depth discussion on advisor compensation), while the tax preparer at the brokerage typically collects an hourly wage or a flat fee per tax form, both of which are normal for that industry. The conflict occurs because the investment advisor might choose investments that make the tax return more complex and therefore more lucrative for the company on the tax side. A perfect example of this is when people invest in publicly traded limited partnerships that require K-1 forms, as Rick and Rachel learned while working with Donna.

A publicly traded company can organize in a variety of types of entities. The most common is a corporation, and most of the companies trading on Wall Street's exchanges are just that. But another type of entity is a limited partnership, which has different tax rules and filing requirements than a corporation. When a publicly traded company decides to use the limited partnership format, it means that people who own shares in that company will have more onerous tax requirements. To help report on those extra tax requirements, limited partnerships create a document for every shareholder—a K-1.

Because accountants and tax preparers typically charge for each tax document they must review or fill out, the fees charged will be lower if the CPA doesn't have to examine any K-1 forms. The opposite is true as well. Buying shares of a publicly traded limited partnership for your portfolio means there will be more tax forms to consider in the tax return, and that will typically increase the revenue collected by the CPA.

None of this is bad. In fact, the main reason for the extra documentation is that the investor is saving on taxes. These forms help to track those details so they can accurately enjoy the tax savings. From this point of view, it's not a very sophisticated idea to make a broad-based ban against owning any publicly traded limited partnerships simply because "I don't want to deal with the K-1s." But it is bad if an investment advisor feels motivated to buy an investment because the company will make more money doing the tax return.

Here's a common scenario where this conflict almost always arises. Whenever investment advisors consider buying an energy-related investment for a client, they are probably examining both publicly traded corporations and limited partnerships. The companies that might be considered could include Exxon, Magellan Midstream, Chevron, Enterprise Products, Shell, and Plains All American. If it's the same team doing the tax return as selecting which of those to buy, there's a real financial benefit if the team selects limited partnerships instead of corporations. For example, Enterprise Products is a limited partnership, and owners of those shares will have to contend with extra K-1 documentation when they do their tax return. The work spent on those extra forms allows the investment advisor's company to charge the client more when preparing the tax return. So the following question is valid: "Is Enterprise Products the right investment for the client, or did the extra tax preparation revenue it creates influence the purchase?"

DISILLUSION

Having the tax preparation and investment advice under the same roof is a clear conflict of interest and a systemic mismatch.

———

The major, nationwide brokerages with their *suitable* legal standard still hiding behind Regulation Best Interest are catering to their salespeople far more than to their paying clients. This systemic truth explains the various conflicts of interest, fee problems, and service issues inherent in Wall Street's brokerage system. Now armed with this knowledge, we can change gears from flaws to solutions. The next chapter illustrates how the system should improve and gives you specific action steps so none of these illusions and systemic inadequacies will fool you in the future.

AVOID THE SYSTEM, AVOID THE PROBLEMS

Action Steps That Put *You* First

hope this book not only empowers everyday investors to understand more about the system in which they are taking part, but also
encourages an open dialogue with my colleagues in the financial
industry. My company, open for business since 2012, was initially an
experiment to test whether or not my ideas about putting the client
first were just ideological naïveté or something more. This last decade
has clearly shown me that if Wall Street would organize every process and operational aspect of its money management service around
customer outreach and fiduciary-level guidance, it's more than just
fulfilling. It's wildly successful.

This approach is why my team grew from zero clients and no
assets to managing about half a billion dollars in less than a decade.

We were ranked on *Financial Advisor* magazine's 2023 list of the largest wealth management firms in the United States and were on *AdvisorHub* magazine's 2023 list of the fastest growing wealth management firms in the United States (#3 in Texas). I understand that in comparison with brokerages and their trillions of dollars under management, our $500 to $600 million is just a drop in the bucket. But that's about $50 million that was entrusted to us each year, so imagine the results if all the advisors at a major, nationwide firm adopted this approach.

Can everyone really win? Absolutely. My experience suggests that the first national Wall Street brokerage firm to leave *suitable* investing fully behind and adopt an enforceable, companywide outreach standard is going to get miles ahead of the competition. Customers will love it, and when one of the larger firms takes that step, here's what that announcement might look like: "All clients, regardless of fees generated for the firm, will receive investment advice under the fiduciary standard and a personal phone call from their financial advisor at least once per quarter."

But until that happens, this chapter describes the action steps you can take to protect your financial security from the flaws discussed in Chapters 7 and 8. Each call to action can be implemented immediately and easily with big impact. It's not difficult to put Main Street on even footing with Wall Street, just like it's not hard to see through an illusion after you understand how the magic trick was done.

The best place to start this story is at the beginning, which is when you hire an advisor. If you hire well, then you won't have to deal with the majority of the Money Magicians' tricks described in the last two chapters, because most of those problems are systemic in nature. If you avoid the system, then you avoid the problems.

ACTION STEP: Don't mix
business with pleasure.

Shouldn't I just work with my uncle since he's a financial advisor?

People will often say that you shouldn't let a close friend or family member handle your finances, and they list two reasons. The first problem that people talk about is the likelihood that your relative will not pay as much attention to your needs because a relative will not be as worried about you becoming dissatisfied. The idea is that because your advisor is your aunt, she will pay attention to other clients ahead of you. Supposedly, this happens because your aunt expects you to be understanding and forgiving of family. I have not seen this in real life, and I disagree that a family member won't give his or her professional best. In fact, I have seen plenty of financial advisors work with friends and family and give their very best. You shouldn't hire a friend or family member, but this "They won't work hard for you" explanation is not a valid reason.

The second problem that people mention is the awkwardness of having someone at the Thanksgiving dinner table that is aware of all your finances. Supposedly, people are incapable of separating work from family fun time. Though I agree you shouldn't hire a friend or family member, I don't think that working with family will ruin the holidays or make regular social encounters difficult.

There's a third problem that no one ever talks about, and it's the one that I believe is the most powerful objection to working with a friend or family member. For you, the client, to accept the advice of your advisor, you need to believe in the person's authority and financial expertise. The reason this is so important is because the unpredictability of the stock market guarantees that there are going to be plenty of difficult investing moments when you will need to have vulnerable conversations about your financial fears and your worries about your portfolio dropping in value. A deep professional trust in the person's financial knowledge is needed to weather those difficult investing climates, and usually, when people hire a college friend or a family member, that strong professional trust isn't there.

Instead, those clients deeply believe in the fact that this person cares for them, which is a different kind of relationship. There will be another serious catastrophe or major crisis on the horizon that will test clients and advisors alike in ways we've yet to imagine. If you hire someone because you believe in the person's investing capability, you'll feel a lot more comfortable in that person's hands during the disaster. When that advisor is giving you guidance that is hard to accept, the foundation of professional respect will be an important pillar to help you successfully navigate that crisis.

But if you hire someone because the person is your cousin or married your sister, that solid professional foundation is missing. It's extremely challenging to accept difficult advice during scary times from someone who you don't truly believe is an investment expert. And since the stock market goes up and down regularly, there's a lot of opportunity for a distance or awkwardness to arise between family members if there's ever any disagreement about how the money has been handled. It's not worth it to risk the loss of a relationship with a friend or a family member over a money-related argument, and that argument is sure to occur if you hire someone based on how much the person likes you or cares about you.

DISILLUSION

The best advisor-client relationship starts as 100 percent professional, and over time (and with consistently excellent service), that professional relationship deepens into an authentic closeness.

ACTION STEP: Ask a tax advisor for help.

What's the right way to find a great financial advisor?

When Rick and Rachel decided to hire a financial advisor, they did an internet search for people nearby and ultimately hired Donna because she was a family friend. That kind of internet search automatically puts the emphasis on the title of "financial advisor," which we've shown in Chapter 7 to be nearly meaningless. What's more, when you do an internet search like that, what you will initially find are the brokerage firms that spend advertising dollars to sponsor themselves to the top of the search results.

It's best to avoid the internet altogether. A much better way to find an excellent investment advisor is to ask your tax advisor or a friend's tax advisor for a recommendation. Because tax advisors must review investment documents as a part of their job, they see valuable information connected to their clients' portfolios. That means they often know the local investment advisors that are doing excellent work growing their clients' portfolios. On the other hand, they also know which investment advisors to stay away from because they are doing a lot of trades, changing brokerages too much, or failing to grow clients' portfolios.

Ask the tax advisor, "Could you introduce me to a fiduciary working at an independent firm focused only on investing and financial planning?" That question highlights the proper title and keeps you away from the major brokerage houses where all the systemic flaws put you at a disadvantage. All the major, nationwide brokerages operate under the *suitable* legal standard, and plenty of independent firms do as well. So going the "indie" route doesn't guarantee the higher legal standard of service. But the independent fiduciary that focuses primarily on investing and financial planning is a powerful combination that puts the client's needs at the forefront.

Another systemic advantage of the independent company is that it does not hold your money directly. You, the client, hold your investments at a discount brokerage (for example, two of America's biggest discount brokerages at the time of this writing are Charles Schwab and Fidelity). You give the independent fiduciary access to your account at the discount brokerage, so it can trade and otherwise supervise your funds. By separating this, you systemically remove the Madoff-style risk discussed in the last chapter. As an example, many of my firm's clients hold their investments at Charles Schwab, and my team has the authority to trade and manage those funds.

With an independent, it's also extremely easy to fire your financial advisor. Since the investment advisor doesn't actually have any of your money, you just take away the person's access to the account. Usually all that takes is a quick phone call to the discount brokerage. That means the account and the investments inside do not move. Nothing changes except who is looking over your investments. That is an important attribute of the professional arrangement because it empowers the client.

What's more, when you align with an independent fiduciary, it's likely the person doesn't have any product bias, meaning he is not incentivized to sell products that the brokerage owns. Because the only product he offers is his investment expertise and planning services, you won't need to wonder if he is suggesting a certain investment because it pays him better. You—the client—are the only one paying him. Since he doesn't accept commissions or kickbacks from third parties, you know that, systemically, he should be focused on just you and your investment requirements.

When you specifically ask for a financial advisor that only does investing and financial planning, you remove much of the systemic conflicts of interest that are built into Wall Street brokerages. If your advisor does not also sell insurance or do tax returns, you've got someone focused on the discipline you've hired him for. When you need an insurance policy or some other financial service, your independent fiduciary will help connect you with professionals who focus specifically on those services.

If you don't have any tax advisor to ask, who else is there to ask? It's hard to just ask a friend or neighbor about a "fiduciary working at an independent." Since the internet will connect you with whoever has the biggest marketing budget (and charges the fees to fill that budget), another way to get a proper answer is to approach your local chapter of Business Networking International (BNI). This networking organization has multiple chapters in major cities and at least one chapter in most small towns. Its goal is to bring different professionals in different careers together to network and help each other grow their business.

A BNI meeting is usually in the morning over breakfast, and anyone can visit. The internet will tell you when and where the members meet near you so you can go for breakfast and get to know the certified public accountant in the group. If there isn't a CPA, you can simply ask the members of the group to refer you to one. BNI has high standards for membership and takes referrals very seriously, so you can rely on this approach to get your process started.

DISILLUSION

Ask a CPA, "Could you introduce me to a fiduciary working at an independent firm known for investing and financial planning?"

ACTION STEP: Hire someone younger than you.

How can you help me to retire if that's when you'll be retiring as well?

If one of your life goals is retirement, then the two or three years before you actually stop working are very important financially. The steps you take during the 36 months before retirement are the final touches to ensure a successful transition to the next phase in life. What's more, the first two to three years in retirement are a critical time in your financial planning because they help set the stage for the level of lifestyle you can expect to enjoy during the rest of your retirement.

The age of your financial advisor plays a big role in the support you receive because you need your investment advisor's best work in the years surrounding your retirement date. Unfortunately, clients often gravitate toward hiring advisors in their own age group since it's easier to connect and get along. The problem with this is, when these clients start to execute a retirement plan, their investment advisors are probably thinking about retirement as well because everyone involved is around the same age. If the advisor is the same age as the client, then the professional relationship is potentially at its most disconnected during those critical retirement years.

A much better arrangement is to align with an advisor who will reach the age of 65 when you have been retired for about 10 years. An easy way to do this is to look to hire someone who is about a decade younger than you. Or you could pick someone in your age group who has an apprentice that you enjoy working with, because that younger professional will likely be doing the majority of the work for you in the future.

DISILLUSION

You need to know your advisor's life plan just as your advisor needs to know yours, because your advisor's retirement date should be at least 10 years after your own.

ACTION STEP: Never pay up front or extra.

I know to avoid commission-based stockbrokers, so isn't that enough?

In Appendix A, you can read the details about how advisors get paid. But no matter which compensation arrangement you select, you don't have to be a financial expert to understand that the longer your money is in your account, the more it is doing good things for you. The sooner your money is removed from your account, the less time it has to earn you interest. That makes the issue of timing very easy. Don't pay up front.

Perhaps the advisor collects her fee once per month, once per quarter, or twice per year; none of that is bad. But it's critical to ensure that the professional charges *in arrears*, meaning "at the end of the period." Wall Street should do the work first and then collect its fee afterward. It's a small client benefit because those dollars stay in your account just a bit longer, but it's a great signal that the organization is systemically paying attention to these smallest of details. When the organization is set up to earn its pay before collecting it, it's more likely the firm's culture will support you and your financial goals in a very meaningful way.

Additionally, you should not pay any extra fees; and while there are a lot of extra fees you can be charged (wire fee, statement fee, online access fee, and most commonly a fee for each trade), there's one simple way to ensure you don't ever have to pay them. Just ask your advisor to email you (and courtesy-copy the compliance manager) the following statement: "I am a fiduciary, and there will never be any other fee connected to your portfolio that I will receive from you or third parties beyond my stated fee schedule, which is attached here." The email is an official communication and a great first step to ensure that whatever fee your advisor charges is the beginning and end of what you must pay them.

This means there are no extra costs for each trade, no extra fees for online usage, nor any additional charges for meetings or report requests. Investment firms that are set up so the client truly pays just the annual fee will have less profit because some of what they collect will go toward covering the cost of trades and other operational needs. But just like collecting a fee *in arrears*, having no extra fees is systemic proof that the company measurably puts serving the client at the forefront of its mission statement.

The most famous "extra fee" on Wall Street is the account closure fee. This is a charge levied against clients when they want to move to a competitor or simply take out all their money and spend it. If the company's policy is that it will charge you a fee to close your account, then don't hire that company in the first place. (See Appendix A for the questions you could ask to help hire the right advisor.) Imagine your future self feeling dissatisfied for whatever reason and wanting to move your investment accounts. Why should you pay the company extra money because it failed to continue to earn your trust and business? Just this one small rule to avoid account closure fees will eliminate all the major brokerage firms because every single one of them charges a fee to close an investment account and transfer to a new brokerage. It's not hard to avoid the system and, therefore, avoid the problems.

DISILLUSION

By refusing to accept extra or up-front charges, clients largely sidestep all the back-out fees and draconian policies that make it difficult for them to hold an advisor meaningfully accountable.

ACTION STEP: Use a personalized financial model to stay focused on the goals that matter to you.

How do I know my investments are doing well?

A professional investment advisor will create and regularly update a financial model for you that is individualized to your situation and your goals. A financial model is a mathematical prediction of what's likely to come. It offers a "what-if" picture of the future and shows you what could happen financially in the years ahead. There are three main questions for which a model should give straightforward answers:

1. How likely is it that I will accomplish my next major milestone or personal goal on time?

2. If I save 10 percent more or less, how does that affect the date I achieve my next major goal?

3. If I spend 10 percent more or less, how does that affect the date I achieve my next major goal?

Using a customized financial model to ensure you're on track to accomplish your goals separates your feelings about the investments from your expectation of achieving your objective. When a fiduciary collects facts about a client's life and inputs them into a financial model, it logically helps that expert examine the probability of success with a focus on reality rather than emotion. Wall Street inserts people's feelings into this process with the risk profile questionnaire mainly because it helps salespeople to sell investments. The Money Magicians are focused on *their success,* which means selling financial products. Independent fiduciaries are focused on *the client's success,* which means creating an excellent financial model that provides valuable information about which path actually leads where the client wishes to go.

When you review the model and maintain it, the model will change the way you understand your money and empower you to stay in control of your finances. This might be a good time to go back and review the illusions described in Chapters 2 and 3 because they trick clients into focusing too much on how much their portfolio is worth. Often, people are trying to keep up with their neighbors or with some index instead of defining their version of success and then aiming directly at it. If you know someone who has said, "I just want as much as possible as soon as possible," or "I see the S&P 500 made 15 percent, so that's what I want to make," then you know someone who has been hijacked by the Money Magicians who need you to keep pushing for more and more while doing a lot of transactions along the way.

If your advisor uses a well-made model to help you to stay focused on your personal goals, you'll know it, because all three of the above questions will be clearly addressed. All the noise surrounding what other people are making (or losing) drops away. For example, if the goal is to pay for a child's education in 18 years, then the model will tell you how much to save each month and whether or not the account is going to be at the goal amount in time. Suddenly, what the S&P 500 earned is a lot less important because no matter how much money you've made or lost, if the answer is, "You're on track," then that can't help but add an important element of calm and logic to the situation.

Remember in Rachel and Rick's story, they were initially asked by Donna to fill out a risk profile questionnaire. She said it was to determine the best investment approach, but insight into how you feel about investing is not the same as a customized financial model. The risk profile questionnaire helps the advisor understand your comfort with investing, but it cannot replace the benefits of an individualized financial model when it comes to empowering the client. A good model will show the client answers to questions like these:

If I saved more, how much faster could I retire?

If I don't buy that beach house, how much could I leave to charity when I pass away?

If I sell the business in five years instead of next year, how does that affect my nest egg when I'm 70 years old?

When can I retire with the greatest probability of success?

How much profit can I reasonably expect to make from my portfolio each year?

A customized financial model should be the focal point of a well-thought-out annual review meeting with an advisor you like and trust. Your advisor could solicit your questions ahead of the meeting and then have the model ready to show you when you meet. In another successful approach, your advisor could share last year's model during the meeting and then collect notes as the two of you discuss how it might be revised. As a follow-up to that discussion, the advisor provides you with those updated answers.

By focusing on your personalized financial model each year, your financial advisor can help you to remove the vague rat-race feeling of trying to beat an index and, instead, focus on your own path and your own needs. Financially speaking, these discussions ensure that you know where you are now and where you intend to go. If it's clear that your train is on time and going in the right direction, you can comfortably release the anxiety associated with what other people's trains are supposedly doing.

DISILLUSION

Expect your advisor to review and update your individualized financial model every year.

ACTION STEP: Expect written notes after every meeting.

Whose job is it to take notes?

After any meaningful meeting or in-depth discussion, you should require that your financial advisor provide you written notes. Like minutes from a meeting, the notes should contain a clear, written description of what was discussed and what the advisor committed to doing for you. This is professionalism at its highest because it puts the client in the position of easily holding the advisor accountable to clear, actionable tasks that all parties agreed would happen.

Providing written notes on important meetings should be a basic staple of every financial advisor's service offering. It's clear proof that the advisor is serious about fulfilling her obligations in a way that the client can appreciate. It also helps to reduce the possibility of misunderstandings because when the client sees the notes, it's a great opportunity to clarify if something's missing or if an idea didn't come through to both parties in the same way.

These notes are not homework or an unnecessary burden to clients because they don't have to read them. The notes from a meeting with a financial advisor are a lot like the gym at a luxury hotel. Customers can go in there and use the weights and treadmill. The equipment is always available and easy to use without any major problem or obstacle. But if clients are not interested in exercising, the hotel doesn't require them to enter the gym. The notes from a financial meeting should be provided to clients in the same spirit. Some clients will want to read them carefully and have more discussions, while others won't even open them up to read them. But the professional provides them every time as a foundational part of her service. See Appendix B for an example of meeting notes from a financial advisor's annual review.

DISILLUSION

Don't work with an advisor who won't put her commitments in writing for you to review and reference again in the future.

———

There are so many great financial advisors out there. It's not hard to find them if you can avoid the brokerage system where the Money Magicians have all the cards. Part Two of this book wasn't about bad financial advisors because, for the most part, investment advisors are good people who want to make a meaningful difference in the lives of their clients. Instead, the second half of this book described the system they find themselves working in and how brokerages, in general, need to change for the better.

CONCLUSION

Today, people are experienced enough with magical tricks that when a magician chooses someone from the audience to help with his act, it immediately sparks a trust problem. Modern audiences know to ask themselves, "Is that person really a stranger, or is this just part of the act?" Because the magician himself is choosing the volunteer, there's a good chance that this supposedly random person has been sitting there the whole time waiting to help with the illusion.

But this insight hasn't come easily. The public has slowly gained this understanding through decades of exposure to magicians in Las Vegas, talent shows on TV, and street performers. Our grandparents had an innocence we no longer possess, which means it used to be easier for illusionists to manipulate their audience's perception.

The process of gaining this same level of insight within financial circles is a journey that's only recently begun. The financial distortions and monetary manipulations in America are as varied as a roster of illusions by a Las Vegas magician. For example, most Americans believe that the Consumer Price Index (CPI) is an accurate measurement of inflation. The problem with this is that the method of calculating CPI has changed more than 20 times since the 1980s. And the people who keep changing it are part of the same government that is deeply in debt and must use the CPI to calculate payments to about 80 million Americans on social security, federal pensions, and other government programs. Can you think of any other situation where people in serious debt get to control how much they must pay?

Just like a magician who won't share his tricks, the actual calculation of CPI is not shared with the public. It's completely hidden, so society is supposed to just trust that the performer onstage who is picking the volunteer isn't pulling the wool over our eyes. But the good news is that just like the famous "saw a woman in half" trick, deceptions like "CPI measures inflation" cannot last forever. The public might still be at the beginning of this learning curve, but the learning is happening and I like to think this book helps that progress continue.

That's why I began with an examination of how Americans save for the future and the misunderstanding behind, "Set it and forget it." Wall Street and the too-big-to-fail banks want us to think that the "it" in this saying is our savings, so that it reads, "Set your savings and forget about saving." But it's supposed to be the opposite. Set your lifestyle so your savings can grow. If we *spend* the same basic amount month after month, then all the extra money we earn over the years can go toward growing our net worth and achieving financial independence. But if we follow their guidance, we will *save* the same basic amount month after month, and then we tend to spend all the extra money we earn. That extra spending means more transactions, which benefit the Money Magicians who thrive on consumerism.

In the second chapter, I reminded readers that financial independence exists because of income, not wealth. We are all bombarded by social pressures to try to achieve a certain level of recognizable wealth and to broadcast our achievements by owning expensive things. Supposedly, if we own a mega yacht or have a 10-car garage filled with Italian sports cars, then we're successful. But the truth is that when we trade our money for a fancy car, we are only showing the world that we used to have money! We don't have it anymore because some of it went to the car salesperson, some went to the car company, and of course, a fair amount went to the government itself. This transaction isn't just costly signaling. It also makes our life more expensive because these new purchases require more money to keep and maintain them. This problem is called "lifestyle creep," and it's a serious issue as each additional purchase erodes our overall financial stability.

The Money Magicians benefit from hiding the power of income so that we focus on things like fancy cars, growth funds, and anything else that doesn't pay you to own it. It suits their purposes well when Americans buy things that pay the owner nothing until another transaction occurs. If you can't get paid until you sell it, then you're going to be plugged into doing the thing that benefits Wall Street and the IRS: a transaction. This is the great misunderstanding of buying collectible coins, cryptocurrency, and non-dividend-paying stocks. The only way you can make money is if you sell the item to someone else for a higher price, assuming someone else will even want to pay more for it than you did. Either way, the Money Magicians love it when you make the sale.

In Chapter 3, I explained the deceptive ways Wall Street measures the growth of our money. I also made the case that it's important to keep a clear view of the income that your wealth creates rather than focus only on the temporary value you might receive if you sell. When we give attention to increasing the income that our wealth creates (instead of just increasing the amount of wealth), then we change our perception of what our money is doing for us. An income-oriented perception, as opposed to average annual return, makes us less prone to panic during difficult times and armors us against the inevitable drops in value that our portfolio will experience in the future.

In the fourth chapter, I demonstrated how Wall Street hides the value of our principal in comparison with our profit. This is particularly evident whenever we reinvest dividends or do rebalancing. Our monthly investment statements and online views of our portfolios are purposefully designed to make sure we see our investments in a way that encourages more transactions and investment activity. The reason the Money Magicians want us to execute transactions is because every time we do, they collect a little more of our money in the form of fees and taxes. This isn't a bad thing by itself, but it's good to realize that constantly transacting is generally beneficial to Wall Street and the IRS.

In Chapter 5, we can see how the IRS positions tax brackets to help hide the most important piece of data in our tax return: how much money we keep after taxes. Instead, we let ourselves get distracted and we end up focusing on how much we're paying the IRS. This plays right into the government's hands because that's who makes the rules about which activities will lower the amount of money the IRS collects. An unfortunate message in this chapter is that most people won't engage politically to meaningfully change taxation rules because it's supposedly easier to do the IRS-approved transactions that lead to deductions.

As people spend their money to try to lower what the IRS gets, they often are lowering the amount of money they get to keep with no strings attached. This is a major disadvantage to the regular citizen, but it's hard to see it that way if the person is convinced that the real goal is to stop the IRS from getting more money. On the other hand, the Money Magicians benefit from the consumerism of buying things to get deductions, because all those purchases help to support a system of taxes on sales, income, and payrolls. A simple and effective way to change this would be to eliminate the contribution limits to our retirement accounts, but that's not even part of the national debate.

In Part Two, I described three specific ways Wall Street needs to improve its offerings to the public. First, it should reject *suitable* investing and embrace the fiduciary standard of service the same way car companies have adopted seat belts and airbags. Suitable investing should feel to Americans like driving drunk or not allowing a woman to open a bank account. While Regulation Best Interest was a small step in the right direction, any true focus on the client's experience demands that suitable investing disappear completely from Wall Street.

Second, brokerage firms should implement firmwide service standards so clients know what they will receive when they hire a financial advisor. It should be the goal of every brokerage firm to make it clear what level of attention its clients will get from the advisors. When clients know exactly what to expect, they can make much better decisions about the professionals they hire. It's also easier to hold those advisors accountable when there's a clear service standard that all parties understand and support.

Lastly, Wall Street should only collect fees from the individual retail customer. It should never charge a back-out fee nor collect fees before it does the work. Just because brokerages disclose a convoluted web of profiteering doesn't mean it's appropriate. It just means they are hiding these questionable practices in plain sight with a mountain of compliance language that no one will ever read.

Perspective is everything. When we see something a certain way, it conveys a particular message. When something—a mirror, an inaccurate measurement, or a costume—comes between us and the things we observe, facts can become less apparent, or they can get hidden away. Conversely, when we recognize the mirrors, make accurate measurements, and remove the costumes, facts can reappear and be even clearer than before. This entire book is about learning to remove the distorting tricks between you and your portfolio.

Frequently, our perception is altered by something that is not in the physical realm. The rules of a card game are a great example. A game's rules are the yardstick we use to perceive how to win and who has lost the contest. In some card games, you want to get as many points as possible, while in others, you need a low score to win. The rules of the game change how you perceive the value of your cards and help you determine which cards you keep and which ones you throw away.

The rules we play by only alter our perception, not reality. When someone at the card table announces a new game, the rules of play change, but everything else for the players stays the same. They have the same deck of cards, the same four suits, the same tabletop, and all the same players. The only thing that's altered is the game itself, but since that changes our perception of what is a wise or foolish card to play, everything that matters has shifted. Our motivation itself is completely redirected. In the first game, we might really want to keep aces in our hand, and with a different set of rules, we'd do anything to get rid of those same cards.

The whole system crumbles into chaos if two people sit down to play cards together but one of them is playing poker and the other is playing Go Fish. The person playing poker will have a set of instructions that show the various poker hands and their rankings. Across the table, the other person playing Go Fish will have a set of instructions that guides him to seek matches. With two separate value systems, the result is the poker player laying down a straight flush and the Go-Fish player laying down a couple of matches. They each think they've won (which is kind of nice, I suppose), but they're not playing together.

This is what happens regularly when Main Street and Wall Street sit down at the table to play investments. Wall Street must adhere to the reporting standards and regulations that support the IRS reporting requirements so that taxes can be properly assessed and collected. We'll call its game "Pay Your Taxes." When you look at your investment statements, you are looking at data specifically lined up to ensure the right amount of taxes get paid to the IRS.

Investors, on the other hand, are playing "Make More Money." They don't want to do anything illegal that avoids taxes, but the purpose of investing, from their point of view, is to grow their financial stability. Make More Money is not the same game as Pay Your Taxes, and *Outsmart the Money Magicians* makes this difference distressingly obvious.

This book has been categorized as "financial education" and is generally recognized for the insight it provides to both investment professionals and beginners alike. While this label is accurate, it is also incomplete. In *Outsmart the Money Magicians*, I've made the case for how Wall Street and the IRS deceive society and encourage us to consume and transact. I've shown how the Money Magicians systemically attend to their own interests before those of the individual investors they are purportedly serving. To accomplish that, I've had to explain *why* the system works as it does. There are always people out there who benefit from things the way they are (which is often why things became that way in the first place). In general, the Money Magicians will not want to lose the benefits they currently receive from being in the powerful position of controlling how we perceive our money. We can expect they will resist change. Make no mistake—this book is just as much an agent for change as it is financial education. Readers won't interact with the Money Magicians in the same way they used to, and the more people who can see through the illusions, the less likely Wall Street and the IRS will continue to perform them.

Understanding how the illusions are created is just the first step. We, the people, should take more responsibility for doing things the hard, proper way instead of the easy, inaccurate way. We, the clients, should demand a clear service model from Wall Street and walk away when Wall Street won't commit to what we want in writing. We, the consumers, should spend less than we earn so that we can hold on to more of our hard-won compensation and, over time, create true financial independence.

Money cannot buy happiness, but it can buy safety and security. It can offer stability and opportunity. Making good decisions with our money is part of being a productive citizen and a good steward at both the individual and the national level. In the financial arena, deception and manipulation erode trust and move us away from the stability and security that are always advantageous to both individuals and society as a whole. The time has come to take the cape and hat from the Money Magicians and lower the curtain on these tricks forever.

THE 14 QUESTIONS TO ASK BEFORE HIRING A FINANCIAL ADVISOR

At the start of my career, I made the decision that I wouldn't work with friends or family in an effort to not take advantage of my closest relationships. One of the first tests of that choice was a relative who asked me to handle her investments. I politely declined and offered her a couple of ideas for how to find another advisor, but she was persistent. Ultimately, I had to interview a number of advisors for her and hold her hand through selecting one. That experience led me to create the following list of questions. What you are about to read is like an insider's guide to probing whether or not an advisor is going to be a great fit for you.

It's important to ask these questions in the order they have been listed because they build on each other in meaningful ways. You don't have to be an expert in finance to use this approach, nor do you need to evaluate the investment acumen of the advisor you're interviewing. Instead, these questions clarify the systemic programs in place so you can be sure you're aligning with a professional whose tools are focused on your success. If you'd like to get these questions in a one-page worksheet that you can fill out during your conversation, please email me at cmanske@manskewealth.com.

You'll notice these questions help to focus the conversation on the service that the advisor offers. The reason is because the service—the disciplined program for taking care of your investments and keeping you informed—is what you are actually paying for when you hire an advisor. People sometimes think that they are hiring an investment advisor to make them money. From that perspective, when the portfolio goes down in value, then that advisor has messed up and should be fired. And the portfolio will go down. Every famous investor has had bad years because there's just no predicting the future. These questions will help ensure you don't fall into the trap of "show me the performance you made last year" to decide if that's the advisor for you.

Another reason these questions focus on the service the advisor offers is to help with another error that people often make, which is this: They want to tell the advisor what they are looking for so that the advisor can listen and then promise that back to them. Instead, you should be gathering the details of what the advisor offers and then you decide if it matches with what you're looking for. Ultimately, these questions will point you toward the advisor's sense of fair play and respect so you can find a professional partner to assist you for many years.

1. What's your full name and the last four digits of your social security number?

You open with this question to gauge the advisor's reaction. You will be sharing all your personal data and your hopes and dreams (not to mention your financial details), so this question allows you a glimpse into the person's respect for the professional relationship that the two of you will be building. You should make note if the advisor seems reluctant to answer.

A second reason to ask this question is because you can use the information to look the professional up online (and the person knows that). A simple internet search for "financial advisor background check" will bring you to sites like FINRA (the Financial Industry Regulatory Authority) and the SEC (the Securities Exchange Commission), which keep tabs on financial professionals and their licenses. Following the prompts at sites like these, you can see if there have been lawsuits or other major complaints lodged against the advisor.

The advisor passes the test if he openly, happily shares with you his details and then, later on, you find that he has a perfectly clean record. The advisor fails this question if he is cagey about answering or if you find his professional record has some nasty surprises. Failing any single question on this questionnaire is a signal to find another advisor. Failing two or more questions is a very strong signal that this is not the advisor for you.

2. How often do you expect we'll see each other face-to-face?

You're asking this question to learn how the advisor provides her services. There's probably no wrong answer except to say, "Well, whenever you'd like to meet," or "How often would you like to get together?" The idea isn't to share with the advisor what you want so she can turn around and offer it to you. The idea is to understand the service the advisor truly offers.

Too often, clients will describe what they are looking for, and then the advisor can just say it back to them. But as the months turn into years, professional investment advisors cannot give every single client unique, special attention. It's not feasible. It's much better for clients to seek to understand what the advisors offer, and if the advisors cannot describe their service in a straightforward manner, then they don't have an answer. And that's a fail for this question. Once armed with a good understanding of their service model, you can choose if an advisor is a fit. Here are some appropriate answers that you might (or might not) like:

"I'd like to see you once every two years."

"I do an annual review for all clients once per year."

"For clients with less than a million dollars, we don't do face-to-face meetings. Above a million dollars, we meet every quarter."

This question is a fail if the description of the service isn't in keeping with what you'd like. It's possible that the service you're looking for cannot be found if you expect the advisor to call you every day and have lunch with you once a week. This would be like a guest at the Ritz Carlton demanding the carpet in the room be a certain color and the pictures on the walls all be of the guest's family. To help manage expectations, I believe my firm offers the highest customer service standards in the industry, meeting each client at least once per year for an annual review.

This question is also a major fail for the advisor if the service itself is not disciplined and clear. Remember in Chapter 6 when Rick and Rachel hired Donna? Donna used mostly email and holiday cards to stay in touch with her clients, which means that Rick and Rachel were surprised when their investments dropped in value and then found it difficult to contact her. Later, their next advisor, Larry, committed to meeting with Rick and Rachel any time they called in to request it. But that still puts the burden of communication on Rick and Rachel.

3. How often do you expect we'll speak with each other?

Just like Question 2 above, the point is to understand the service the advisor is offering. A wrong answer is anything that is not well defined or is difficult to understand. For example, "Oh, I pride myself on staying in touch with my clients. You'll hear from me whenever something important arises." This is not a service model; it's a vague description of the advisor's intentions.

Here are appropriate answers that might not match up with what you're looking for, which is fine. The point is that they are clear descriptions of when you can expect to hear from your investment professional:

> "You probably won't speak with me all that often, as I have staff that handle day-to-day client affairs. They will email you at least four times a year."

> "I personally call all my clients every quarter."

> "For clients with less than a million dollars, we reach out once per year. Above a million dollars, we will call you every three months."

The advisor fails this question if the description of the service isn't in keeping with what you are looking for. I once knew a prospective client who asked if I would be willing to call her each week to answer questions about things she'd received in the mail. It was great she had a clear idea of the service she was looking for, and it helped us to realize that we weren't a good fit. To help manage expectations for this question, an extremely high standard for outreach would be monthly. At my own firm, we call Every Client, Every Month™ and aim to return all calls and emails before the end of the next business day.

And just as with Question 2 above, the advisor does not pass if the service itself is not disciplined and clear. A good service model is simply the description of whatever outreach you, the client, can expect from that professional. It should be easy to understand and clearly described on the company website. When you can properly evaluate the service you will receive, it's a lot easier to compare one advisor with another. The following are three examples of basic service models:

> "I will reach out to you twice a year by phone or email, and after your portfolio has grown to over $2½ million, I will reach out to you once per quarter."

> "All advisors at Super Financial connect with clients via email at least once per year on their birthday to ask them to

come in so we can present an annual review of the portfolio to them."

"If you hire me, my assistant will be your first point of contact, and she will call you every quarter, just like she does for all my other clients."

After reading the three examples above, you might be thinking, "I probably would want more attention than what all three of those advisors offer." Your reaction is exactly what would happen if Wall Street offered clients a clear service model. Each customer could make an informed decision when hiring an advisor, and with that clarity, it's a lot easier to hold the professional accountable in a meaningful way during the engagement.

You should never hire an advisor that says, "I'll call if something comes up." Newspapers are published every day because "something comes up" on an hour-by-hour basis. Beware if you hear, "If you need something, just call. I'm glad to help." This means the burden of communication in the relationship is on the client, and systemically, it needs to be the other way around. You are paying the advisor to give you attention, so the least the advisor can do is clearly describe how much attention you'll get.

4. How quickly do you respond to a phone call that you've missed?

This addresses a basic truth in any service: People call in, and the advisor is busy in a meeting, is on the other line, or may be out sick. The point is, sometimes you will want to talk to her, and she won't be immediately available. How long do you have to wait? Like Question 1, this also is testing the advisor's openness and willingness to serve you, because a top-notch professional will have a reasonable, straightforward answer. But sometimes the advisor can get defensive or question why you'd ask this question, which is a red flag.

An appropriate answer is something like, "I call back that business day or the next business day." An inappropriate answer sounds like this: "Well, why do you ask? Hmmm, that's a good question.

What sounds right to you?" If the advisor is at all evasive or cagey in response to this question, she probably doesn't have the kind of service model you're looking for.

5. How does my tax advisor fit into all this?

This is a strong question because it's a basic requirement for an excellent investment advisor to liaison with the client's tax advisor. The tax advisor is arguably more important to the client than the financial advisor because of the reasons listed at the end of Chapter 5. Therefore, it's important to ensure that your financial advisor's service model includes regular communication with your tax advisor.

There are many ways the two experts work to the client's advantage, but the biggest ones focus on checks and balances. First, there's a level of professional oversight that automatically happens when two separate professionals cooperate with informal professional courtesy. The financial advisor knows his work will be seen by the tax advisor, and the tax advisor knows her work will be seen by the financial advisor. It helps to increase the probability that nothing untoward will happen to the client.

Second, by having two separate sets of eyes looking at your financial picture from two different angles, it helps to decrease the probability of mishaps and mistakes. Because your investment advisor sees what is happening taxwise for all his clients, he's more likely to notice when your tax picture has something in it that looks unusual. The same occurs in the other direction because the tax advisor sees what is happening investmentwise for all her clients. When either of them sees something that doesn't look familiar, the two professionals can collaborate to your benefit.

There are many ways an investment advisor can keep a tax advisor informed, so all you need to look out for is the lack of a process. If the person you are interviewing cannot clearly describe how he liaisons with his clients' tax advisors, then this is probably not someone with a disciplined service model. Some failing answers are, "Would you like me to call your tax advisor?" or "I'm not a tax advisor, and we don't do taxes."

A passing answer would be one that shows the advisor has a program in place to keep all clients' tax advisors informed so that the investment strategy works in tandem with the tax strategy. You don't have to be a financial expert to know when an advisor doesn't have a process to keep tax advisors informed. And the same goes for when the advisor clearly does have one. Here's an example: "I will reach out to your tax advisor in the first 90 days that we work together to get permission to share information. Then, each year, I have three major outreaches I do to keep your tax advisor in the loop. One of them is to give your tax advisor your tax documents in connection with the work we're doing here. The second one is to share your financial plan with your tax advisor to get any tax-oriented feedback. And the final one is to discuss tax loss harvesting and if we can lower your taxes each year by doing tactical transactions for you."

6. What is your account review like, and may I have a copy of your typical account review agenda?

Every advisor will have a different way of doing account reviews, which are a staple offering where you meet with your advisor and discuss your investments and your individualized financial model. You don't have to be an expert trying to determine which account review approach is the best. Instead, this is a pass/fail arrangement like all the questions in this list. If the professional doesn't have an agenda that already exists and can easily be shared with you right that moment, then the person is probably just winging it and not truly taking the review of client accounts seriously. In the last 20 or so years, I've given this list of questions to hundreds of people and have gotten some interesting feedback on this question.

It seems a lot of advisors will cover up that they don't have a written process for how to handle a client's annual review by saying, "That's proprietary information, and I'm not permitted to give it out." Or they will say, "Our compliance department won't let me give that to you." This is a fail for the question.

They are in the business of doing financial planning and giving investment advice. They will have to repeatedly address certain things on a regular basis (maybe once a year, once a quarter—again, no wrong answer except to not have a model at all). To not have a check-list of those items is unprofessional. What items would you find on an annual review agenda? Things like checking beneficiaries, checking on your goals to see if they've changed, and of course reporting to you on your investments and the current economic environment. Again, you don't have to evaluate the agenda itself, just ensure the person has one.

7. How often do you expect you'll come to my home or office?

This question helps to identify an advisor who doesn't have a mature practice yet. In this case, the person is much more likely to answer, "I'll come to your home or office any time," and that's truly a wrong answer because it's not sustainable. At some point, she will have enough clients and enough work that she cannot be in her car driving around town every day. She needs her clients to come to her.

This question is a pass if the advisor gives a clear answer like, "I only do meetings outside the office for my elderly clients who cannot come into the office." Or another possible answer is, "I will meet you at your home or office for our first annual review, but then after that, we'll do reviews at my office or over videoconference." Perhaps you don't like these answers, and that's a good thing! With a clear response, you can gauge if the service is in keeping with what feels right to you and your goals. But beware when the answer is, "What feels right to you? I can accommodate."

8. What financial designations do you have?

The Certified Financial Planner® (CFP®) designation is the preemi-nent accolade for the investing and financial planning industry. There are high ethical standards for CFPs that help to guard you, the client, from bad actors. People in a career focused on personal financial plan-ning and investing will have this designation if they are taking their offering seriously. If the advisor you are talking to does not have that designation, then it's a fail.

There are a lot of other credentials and short little courses that give advisors designations and specialties. You don't have to know all those designations (and there are a lot of them). You just need to be on the lookout for one: the CFP. It's a board certification that is monitored and renewed every two years by passing various tests and meeting continuing education requirements. Without it, you're talking to someone who, for whatever reason, hasn't gone deep enough in his career or just doesn't value the client's experience enough to offer that level of expertise.

9. How many people directly support you or are on your staff?

If the answer is, "I have an assistant," then that's a fail. This isn't a western movie, and no advisor is the Lone Ranger. If the person you are interviewing is the only investment expert on the team, then there's going to be a problem because you're hiring someone without systemic depth. People get tricked into this because they think, "You are an employee at a big brokerage firm, so you have a lot of people backing you up." But that's not the case. The brokerage culture is very "dog-eat-dog," and the advisors don't typically help each other.

Remember, you are hiring this person to help you with goals that could be decades away. Over that long timeline, some unique and difficult challenges may arise. If the advisor gets hospitalized for a while, how will your portfolio be cared for? Systemic depth is important, and you're looking for at least two accomplished investment advisors on the team.

10. What type of investments do you use most often for your clients?

Let the advisor talk. Listen to how she answers this question. Do you feel like you are being talked down to? Has she turned into a teacher on a stage, and you're the student in the classroom? Or do you feel she is comfortably chatting with you about money? You don't have to understand investing to know if you enjoy the interaction. The main reason you are hiring the person is to talk to you about money. If you don't like how it feels right now, why do you think that will change?

There is a wrong answer to be wary of, and that's the nonanswer—such as, "Well, what investments are you comfortable with?" or "I use pretty much everything." If the advisor isn't actually answering the question, then how can you expect to get straightforward answers later when she's already earned your business?

11. How are you compensated?

Overall, there are two basic ways to pay financial advisors. One is by commission, and the other is by an asset-based fee. The commission is a payment received at the time of the trade. If no trades happen, then the advisor does not collect any compensation. It's not that this arrangement is bad or evil; it's just that, structurally, the commission aligns the advisor *against* the client. Each time the advisor brings an idea to the client, the client logically must ask, "Is this really a good thing for me, or does my broker need to pay his utility bill."

Commission-based, brokerage salespeople only make money if the client agrees to buy or sell an investment in her portfolio. That means the client is compensating the salesperson for his *ability to influence*. It doesn't matter if the investment is good or bad because the advisor will get paid either way at the time of the trade. What matters, financially speaking, is if the salesperson can convince the client to act.

For example, if the broker calls to say a client should buy ABC Fund, then the client must ask herself if ABC Fund is really in her best interest. It's highly possible that the broker is only legally required to suggest investments that are suitable, so it's OK if the investment is extremely expensive or otherwise wouldn't meet the fiduciary legal standard (as described in Chapter 8). If the client agrees to buy it and then ABC Fund goes up, the broker could call to say, "We made money. Let's sell and buy something else," which is a trade that creates more compensation. If ABC Fund goes down, the broker could call to say, "This isn't going the way we want. It's a good thing I'm watching it for you. Let's get out before you lose too much. I'll sell this and buy something else for you." The commission-based broker benefits from market fluctuation, because whether up or down, the next step is more trades. And more trades mean the broker collects more pay.

Opposite the commission, the fee-based approach ties the advisor's compensation to the performance of the accounts. In this case, the payment is received each month or quarter regardless of the number of trades done, because this fee is based on the value of the account. When the advisor suggests an investment, there's no additional compensation for that advisor unless the investment results in an increased portfolio value. Structurally, this fee aligns the client and the advisor because they both want the account to go up in value.

For example, if an advisor charges 1.25 percent (which is about in line with industry averages), then an account with $100,000 in it will pay him $1,250 per year if nothing changes. If the advisor makes investments that increase the account value, then 1.25 percent of that bigger value means a pay raise for him. The opposite is true as well. When the investments do poorly, the system automatically holds the advisor accountable because his 1.25 percent of the smaller amount is a pay cut.

Think for a moment about your own monthly pay, and imagine that suddenly, you make 20 percent less. It's a big deal, right? That kind of pay cut affects your fee-based financial advisor in the same way, which is why fee-only advisors are typically seen as higher-quality professionals who focus on the skill of investing as opposed to the skill of sales and influencing.

Unfortunately, fee-based advisors can also do nothing except play golf all day and still collect compensation on the accounts they've been entrusted to supervise. This is another reason why your advisor should provide a clear service model. You aren't paying the fee for the promise of making more money because no one can make guarantees like that. Instead, that fee buys the advisor's time, attention, and financial expertise. The way you know you will like how you receive the advisor's attention and expertise is by examining his service model with the questions in this list.

So back to the question of how the advisor is compensated, the trick to avoid almost every problem described in this book is to go with a fee-based, independent fiduciary for your serious money. If you like the service model, then you'll only have to worry about two things related to compensation, and both can be taken care of with this question. The first one is timing, which should be "in arrears," meaning the advisor collects his fee after he does the work. And the second one concerns extracurricular fees, and there shouldn't be any. No extra cost for trading, statement delivery, online access, updating a financial model, etc.

12. If your office found out that I had a death in the family, what would you do?

A good financial advisor would likely answer this question with something like, "Well, if I knew the person who died, I'd attend the funeral. I'd probably get flowers. I'd ring you to see if I can do any-thing for you. If you needed something—anything—you could count on me." But an *excellent* financial advisor wouldn't say any of those things. An investment expert at the top of her game would answer with a focus on the professional service that you are paying for, not the offer of friendship and flowers.

An expert's answer would sound something like, "I've helped clients in that situation before. I would examine your account's ben-eficiaries to see if there needs to be any updates. If there are any cash flow problems related to the death, I would help to ensure bills get paid. I also would check to see if you need assistance with collect-ing life insurance proceeds." These are real work-related solutions to a serious financial dilemma, namely the loss of a family member. Sending flowers to the funeral is a basic kindness and shouldn't be offered as a reason for you to hire someone.

13. May I have a list of references please?

If an advisor cannot give you a list of references, then this is a major fail. Over the years, I've heard where other advisors have answered this question with something like, "My clients' information is private," or

"My compliance department won't allow me to share that information with you." This really does not pass the commonsense test.

Imagine that you are a client of an advisor, and you think very highly of her. You have loved working with her and hope to continue the relationship for many more years. If she called you and asked if she could give out your name and number in the event that someone wanted a reference, you'd say yes. If the person doesn't have three to five people who will sing her praises for her, then you owe it to yourself to hire a different advisor.

14. Will you please email me stating that you are legally a fiduciary and that you'll contact me in the ways you've just described? Please courtesy-copy your compliance manager in case I need to reach out to that person in the future.

This final question allows the advisor to put the discussion in writing and introduces you to the person that matters if ever you need to make a complaint. If the advisor cannot commit in writing to what he said, then that's a strong signal to go with a different advisor. Don't sign anything or move forward until you've received this email and you like what it says. If all's well, you can respond to both the advisor and the manager with a simple, "Wonderful! I'm ready to sign the documents and begin working with you."

EXAMPLE OF NOTES FROM A MEETING SENT VIA EMAIL

Dear Rick and Rachel,

Thanks for making the time for our recent annual review—I think it was a great discussion. As you know, whenever we do annual reviews or face-to-face updates, I send the notes from the meeting to you within three business days of the discussion. I hope it helps to keep you informed and keep us all on the path toward the accomplishments that truly matter to you.

We typically suggest sharing information like this with our clients' tax advisors, so please consider sending this information on or let us know if we have your approval to do so for you. Speaking for all of us here on the team, we sure do appreciate your continued trust, and I am especially thankful if you mention my name to others. The vast majority of the work I do is for "windfall" scenarios: life insurance received after a death; lawsuit settlements: cash value created by an IPO; consolidations at retirement; inheritance; sale of a business; even gambling winnings. I've found that these folks really appreciate my introduction because they have an immediate need for someone in my field, especially if they were not already comfortable with seven-figure portfolios. OK, here are the notes as promised!

Regarding Personal Items

- You provided me with a good look at what is happening for you, especially as it relates to your personal financial goals.

- You gave me insight into some of your extracurricular pursuits. I am looking forward to trying a few of the restaurants you recommended.

- We talked about general hopes/expectations. I got a great glimpse of your family and immediate hopes for the future—thanks!

- You explained that your next big milestone is possibly leaving Texas for a job in Florida, but there's a slim chance this will actually occur.

- We confirmed you've got my number in your cell phone so you can easily reach my office.

Regarding Investment Items

- We talked about our thoughts on how interest rates rising, taxes rising, and the value of the dollar declining are important pieces of the puzzle right now.

- We discussed your investments and the level of diversification involved with the overall portfolio.

- We agreed to take advantage of market highs by selling some of the more profitable securities in your accounts.

- You'd like a professional second opinion on your whole-life policies—feel free to share those statements via email.

- We agreed to try to be "buyers" if there's a market pullback, specifically using a dollar cost averaging strategy over the next 12 to 18 months.

- We discussed our concerns that markets seem overly sensitive to legislative influence and international news.

- We went over the return of your portfolio, and you expressed satisfaction.

- We went over your recent statement and discussed how you can use it to keep your pulse on the portfolio.

- We went over two companies, AMD and MRO—I provided research from three sources on each.

Regarding Goals and Milestones—Short-Term Goals

Q1 2024: Finish your interviews and decide on a new insurance agent.

Q2 2024: After deciding, please feel free to share the policy paperwork before you sign so my team can provide comments.

Q3 2024: My team will refer you to some estate planners so you can interview them.

Q4 2024: Hire an estate planner and get your wills/trusts in place.

Regarding Goals and Milestones—Repeating Annual Goals

January: Meet with your financial advisor for your annual review, and go over long-term financial plan and personalized investment model.

February: Provide your financial advisor with statements from your 401(k) plans and all other investment accounts that our team does not directly supervise so we can ensure all your monies are working together.

February: Provide your tax advisor with documents to help complete tax return (we will do that for your investment accounts).

March: Complete your taxes.

April: Personal family meeting to discuss your annual lifestyle. How much do you spend each month? Is this working well?

May: Annual physical with the same doctor/team each year.

June: Home maintenance month (major systems all checked like AC units, pool equipment, water heaters, etc.).

July: Your annual vacation.

August: Car maintenance month (turn them in for service).

September: Family safety month (inspect safety kits; check emergency supplies; do a fire drill).

October: Meet with your tax advisor to ask, "How can I do things differently to lower my taxes?"

November: Personal family meeting to discuss what the future holds. How will you get there?

December: Make goals for next year.

Regarding Goals and Milestones—Long-Term Goals

2025: Your child graduates from high school.

2027: Buy a new car, and drive it until 200,000 miles.

2029: Your child graduates from college.

2029: You expect your next promotion.

2030: Review your personal insurance policies with an expert, and update/change as appropriate.

2030: Revise your estate plan every seven to ten years.

2031: The house should be paid off—time for a "no more mortgage" party!

2032: Have a candid conversation with all heirs about what you expect after you are gone.

2033: Retirement path: Six years until the date, begin changing the portfolio slightly to create income.

2034: Retirement path: Five years until the date, look at paying off all debt prior to.

2035: Retirement path: Four years until the date, consider buying new cars and updating home.

2036: Your first child is likely to be married around this time.

2036: You wanted to redo the kitchen around this time.

2036: Retirement path: Three years until the date, look at your monthly lifestyle number—accurate?

2037: Retirement path: Two years until the date, portfolio now creates the income needed in retirement.

2038: Retirement path: Test the waters—live the lifestyle like you're retired—everything worked out?

2038: Retirement path: Meet with someone from Social Security and other relevant government agencies for information/guidance.

December 31, 2038: Retirement date.

2040: Milestone achieved: Celebrate your sixty-fifth birthday.

Regarding Professional/Administrative Items

- We talked about your beneficiary picture, and we're glad to help make it easy to update that accordingly.

- You agreed that your online access was working well.

- We discussed my service, and you indicated all was as you wanted.

- We didn't specifically mention it while together, but it's really great you both chose to come for the discussion—it truly helps me to plug in to what's important to you.

Regarding My Commitments

- I have plans to conduct an annual review with you again this time next year at the very latest.

- I promised to complete a review of your 401(k) plan so you can maximize that program.

- I expect my office will be in touch monthly over the next year in accordance with our mantra, Every Client, Every Month™.

- We'll update your listed beneficiaries using the documents you completed while together.

- I promised to combine the two single-name accounts for you.

- Once you email me the statements, I'll provide a professional second opinion on your whole-life policies.

- I offered to complete the cost basis records for your Merck and Exxon holdings.

- I committed to reaching out to your friends, Carrie and Jeff, to help them with their company 401(k) plans at no cost—thank you for mentioning my name to them.

Conclusion

Please let me know if there's anything in these notes that you'd like to go over again or if you think we need to realign to more current/applicable plans. Many thanks!

Gratefully,
Chris

ACKNOWLEDGMENTS

I feel a great appreciation for the help, guidance, and friendship of Michele Matrisciani. I'm very proud to be associated with her and the McGraw Hill publishing house. With her editing and organizing prowess, I'm convinced this final product is light years ahead of where I'd be without her warp-speed engines helping me along.

To my agent, Francesca Minerva, thank you for your belief in me and for not giving up on the idea that I might have a second book in me. Your expertise and great sense of humor have been a gift for which I'm very grateful.

To Christopher Brown, Scott Sewell, Jonathan Sperling, Maureen Harper, and Pattie Amoroso, I say thanks for your guidance and attention to my book as McGraw Hill made its changes and transitions. I'm extremely grateful to each of you, and to Christopher and Scott particularly for sharing your overall publishing and marketing expertise.

Patricia Wallenburg, you are a wonderful professional who I never got to shake hands with but am convinced we'd be best friends. Your production skills are topnotch, and my book is so much better for your contributions. Thank you!

Patricia Bernstein and Maria Piazza from Bernstein & Associates are so kind, witty, sharp, and a joy to work with. The introductions they made for me in the public relations world were instrumental in getting the word out about this book. I cannot say, "Thank you!" enough to them for finding/opening so many doors for me and then helping me to walk through them with my best foot forward.

To my family and friends at work, you've been such a support and inspiration. Zach Welborn, Elijah Lopez, and Chance Burroughs—and especially Lien Busby—I consider you my second family and can't wait to see what's next for us personally and professionally. I appreciate all the lessons you've each provided and the opportunities you've helped us seize together.

My parents, Robert and Rise Manske, have always been an important source of support, and I'm grateful for their guiding hands all these years.

At home, my four daughters give my life meaning and my wife gives my life fulfillment. I appreciate your support of all my o'dark-thirty wake-ups so I could log in and continue writing, revising, and other keyboard gymnastics. I wore your hats, welcomed your 6 a.m. hugs, drank your hot chocolates, typed during your music lessons, stretched out with you, got to speak at your campus . . . and love you, love you, love you. "I love you," is an easy thing to say, and some say it incessantly, so thank you family—especially Jess—for truly showing me the power and permanence of that phrase.

INDEX

of third-party money managers,
133–134
transaction, 133, 199–200
up-front, 152–154, 190–191,
201
(*See also* Costs)
Fidelity, 188
Fiduciaries at independent
companies, 187–189
Fiduciary standard, 167, 169,
184, 187, 200
Financial advisors, 141–159
back-out fees of, 154–155
as brokerages' legal representatives, 142–143
conflicts of interest for,
141–142, 146, 150–152
customers as products for,
155–159
expertise of, 145–149
fiduciaries at independent
companies, 187–189
friendship offered by, 158
hiring (*see* Hiring advisors)
minimum account sizes for,
175–176
plan for avoiding problems
with (*see* Action steps for
investors)
projected cash flow reports
from, 38–41
quotas of, 143–145
semantics obscuring responsi-
bilities of, 142–143
system limitations for, 141–142
typical experiences with
(*see* Working with financial
advisors)
up-front charges of, 152–154
written meeting notes from,
195–196, 219–225
(*See also* Investment advisors;
Tax advisors)

Financial illusions, ix–x, xii, 1,
3–5 (*See also* individual
illusions)
Financial models, 192–195
The Financial Samurai (Dogen), 35
FiscalData.Treasury.gov, 117
Flat tax, 119
FOMO (fear of missing out), 40

Gains:
and percentage of income
received based on original
investment, 96–97
reported, actual profit vs.,
86–89
and reporting that gives
appearance of loss, 80–84
and sense of fairness, 103–106
your gains vs. IRS tax gains,
84–86, 92–93
(*See also* Profit)
Geometric mean, 59–60
Goals:
accomplished in spite of feelings, 171–172
losing sight of, 103–106, 108,
113
personalized financial model
focusing on, 192–195
Griffin, Kevin, 35
Guess the Number game, 47–50
Guth, Werner, 104

Hall of Mirrors trick, 24–26
Hester, Tanja, 35
High-risk investments, 64
"High-water mark" for savings
account, 19–20
Hiring advisors, 130–131
independent fiduciaries,
187–189
questions to ask before,
205–218

fees of, 133, 199–200
by third-party money managers,
133
when advisors change firms,
156, 158
Traveling Wallet (Neacato), 35
Trust in advisors, 185–186
2 Frugal Dudes (Griffin and
Merron), 35

Ultimatum Game, 103–106, 108,
111–116, 118–121
Up-front charges, 152–154,
190–191, 201
USASpending.gov, 117
USDebtClock.org, 117

Value-added tax, 119
Variable lifestyle, 3, 12–16
Volatility, 64–66

Wall Street, x, xi, xii, 143, 202
Wealth, 23–45
correcting the illusion of,
30–42
and divorce settlements for
stay-at-home spouses, 44–45
financial system trick with,
26–27
income vs., 26–27, 198–199
and magician's illusion, 24–26

and net worth vs. income,
23–30 (*See also* Investment
performance)
and "profit-by-sale" mentality, 4
in real life, 27–30
reflections of, 16, 24, 26, 28–30
as using potential of money, 34
Withdrawals, accounting of,
66–71
"Wizard of Oz effect," 148
Working with financial advisors,
129–140
brokerage products, 138–139
changing advisors, 138, 139, 156
commissions, 136
fees of third-party money
managers, 133–134
hiring advisors, 130–131
and initial public offerings,
134–135
questioning fees, 135–136
second opinions, 136–137
tax implications of actions,
137–138

Yield:
bond, 75–76
on investment statements,
99–100
on original investment, 96–97
principal-focused, 100

ABOUT THE AUTHOR

Christopher Manske, CFP®, is on a mission to improve finance for everyone. A US Military Academy graduate, he left the Army as a captain, joined Merrill Lynch, and grew his investment group so fast that he was selected to help create and deliver financial training nationwide. He founded Manske Wealth Management in 2012, and his firm has been repeatedly recognized by *Financial Advisor* magazine as one of the nation's largest investment  firms. In 2023, *AdvisorHub* magazine listed Chris Manske among the fastest-growing advisors in the country. Manske's thoughts can be seen in the *Wall Street Journal, Texas Monthly, Forbes, Yahoo! Finance*, and many more. He's been a keynote speaker for the AARP, and his team has addressed many major companies including Microsoft, IBM, Exxon, Boeing, and GE. For over 20 years, he's been married to a Texas Aggie named Jessica, and together they raise four daughters.